# Kwajalein,

## An Island Like No Other

Lynn A Jacobson

Illustrations by R. Meimei Pan

ISBN: 1491007583
ISBN 13: 9781491007587

# Previous books published by author

## Surviving Five Daughters

Note: Survival, yes.  Recovery, still in doubt.

## Secrets of A Trophy Husband

(Things We Do For Love)

Note: My wife's favorite book.

# Dedication

To Meimei Pan, who has now survived the arduous and unenviable position of being a companion-deprived author's wife—not once but three times. I hope her ongoing support means she loves me as much as I love her, rather than indicating she is just trying to keep me out of trouble and off the streets.

I dedicate the first chapter to my grandson, Nick Rice, who is the biggest fan of my shark chapters.

# Acknowledgments

The daunting task of my completing a third book owes much to my Palo Alto Avenidas writing group and the friends and relatives who dared read, comment on, and edit early versions of this book. Fan Maureen Kelland and niece Jentien Pan were the first two brave adventurers to plow through the entire manuscript.

Raelyn Jacobson, Daughter 5, and my wife, Meimei Pan, rambunctiously, ruthlessly, and relentlessly took no prisoners in their editing and proved that the C and D grades I received in English classes were overly generous. The battles in my family over the use of dashes and commas (the 'Comma Sutra Wars') were particularly fierce. My wife's illustrations and Tienlyn, Daughter 4, Photoshop guru, brought my collection of old photos and maps to life.

Phil Monson, a Kwajalein coworker with whom I shared many experiences, contributed both photos and stories; Gary Campbell made several suggestions, which ultimately evolved into full fledged chapters; Glen Williamson's story was the foundation of "Don't Make Waves." David Gjerdrum was master of facts, and Richard Graglia illustrated the fishing dogs story. If you add all those who played roles in producing the final product, it becomes unclear to me why I was even needed.

Thanks to you all, Lynn
March, 2014

# CONTENTS

# Illustration Index

# Foreword

Someone had to write this book. I finally got tired of waiting—so here it is.

The stories contained in this book are based on my experiences gained from five years (spread over three tours between 1964 and 1972) of living and working on Kwajalein, a nine-hundred-acre island in the Marshall Islands. Kwajalein is situated 2,450 miles west of Honolulu and 600 miles north of the equator and has served as the US downrange missile-test-site terminus since 1962. I've included several contributions from a few fellow Kwaj-ites who were gracious enough to share their stories with me. My ultimate goal in writing this book was to capture the essence of life on Kwajalein in sixty-two nearly autonomous chapters and as such many of the details and dates are only approximates.

Kwajalein was and is an island like no other in so many ways—so many unique happenings, so many "only on Kwajalein" events. Too isolated, too small, too few women, too secret, too low (average elevation under seven feet), too much money...

## AN ISLAND LIKE NO OTHER

Normal life, as we know it, is covered in so many protective veneers and trappings that it is very difficult to analyze or even partially understand. It's like an archeological site of an ancient civilization—you know there is so much there; but its secrets are not forthcoming without a great deal of digging.

Now remove the top dozen levels of debris, and much more becomes clear. Kwajalein is like an ancient site that has been partially excavated, where many of life's challenges and modern trappings have been removed—what is left comes into focus and can be observed more closely.

## An Island Like No Other—Isolation

There are no major population centers within two thousand miles: Honolulu, Hawaii, is 2,450 miles away; Auckland, New Zealand, is 3,140 miles; Brisbane, Australia, 2,650 miles; Tokyo, Japan, 2,560 miles. Even Guam, the nearest population center of over seventy-five thousand (in the mid-1960s), is 1,380 miles distant.

The only transportation off island during my tours was a twice-a-week eight-hour charter flight to Honolulu, since sea transportation was virtually nonexistent.

First-class mail delivery took seven days, and a single long-distance phone line was available only for businesses and emergencies. The ham-radio operators tried to fill in as much as they could, but usually conditions were so contaminated with static that only personnel from the Philippines could take advantage of this link to the outside world (some aspects of the Tagalog language seem to enhance communication more effectively than English in noisy environments).

Kwajalein did have a radio station but no TV. The island's newspaper, *The Hourglass*, published a limited amount of mostly local happenings and only a smattering of mainland news.

Isolation, isolation, isolation.

## An Island Like No Other—Culture Groupings

Four cultures met on Kwajalein—they interacted yet did not clash, but then, they didn't particularly blend either. Each had its own values, its own style, and its own ways of doing things. They cooperated because it made everything run more smoothly, not because it was natural.

First and most importantly—for without them the other three groups wouldn't be needed—there was the scientific community of about two thousand, including dependents, comprised mostly of highly educated engineers and scientists who tended to be oblivious to class status. In his book, *The Status Seekers*, Vincent Packer mentioned engineers but only in passing. He concluded that as a group, they were effectively outside class structures. Scientific research thrives in a classless society where decisions are based primarily on facts rather than opinions.

In contrast, the army, which controlled the nonscientific logistics and general security on the island, *required* class distinction, as following orders was paramount. Wars are not won by troops second-guessing their officers. Following orders, however, does tend to stifle creative thinking. An unavoidable consequence of their stratified-status environment was that the wife of a major not only knew the other wives of majors but was also aware of the exact date each husband had last been promoted—a date which determined her own relative seniority.

The third group was comprised of support workers on bachelor status, mostly from Hawaii,, who made up 60 percent of Kwajalein's general population. Equivalent to the noncommissioned officers in the military, they were the heavy lifters when it came to making the nonscientific aspects of Kwajalein work.

The fourth culture was that of the Marshallese, the citizens of the host country. Their culture evolved to enable them to successfully weather drought, typhoons, and other hardships. Sharing and self-reliance, especially within the *bwij*, the extended family from the mother's side, were their basic survival tools. (Clans were comprised of a collection of several *bwijs*.) Time wasn't important but directions were—they were experts in reading the ocean. They practiced matrilineal succession where power was held by males (the *alap* was the chief or most senior elder of a *bwij*) but was inherited via the eldest female. It was the cousin with the oldest mother who was next in line to inherit power (see chapter 24).

## AN ISLAND LIKE NO OTHER—MONEY

At all skill levels, incomes were high, except for the military personnel and a handful of government workers. Bonuses, six-day weeks (overtime), and incentive pay scales were the primary perks that drew workers to Kwajalein. Net income was further enhanced either by per diems or equivalent housing and food allowances. As a final kicker, US income taxes took effect for only a few of the highest-paid personnel, and in most circumstances, there was no obligation to pay state income tax. During my second tour, the Marshallese government did come to the realization that they could tap into an additional source of revenue by passing their own income tax laws. Initially it didn't begin until an individual earned $20,000, which just happened to hit most of the Kwajalein workers but none of the Marshallese. After my third tour, however, the Marshallese tax rate was raised, and the minimum income eligibility limit was lowered several times.

## An Island Like No Other—Recreation

Recreation was one area in which Kwajalein shone. Scuba diving, including compressed air, dive boat transport, and a free lunch, ran $2.90 a month. Diving visibility was over eighty feet, and shells and exotic fish were plentiful. Deep-sea fishing was free and beach combing productive.

The flying-club costs were reasonable (no aviation fuel tax), and golf, swimming pools, the beach, sailing, and tennis were all free. Tuition for the University of Hawaii extension classes was also quite low.

On top of all these benefits, drinks at all the clubs were super cheap, as there was no liquor tax.

## An Island Like No Other—Women (or Lack Thereof)

Three thousand bachelors dripping in cash—and no women to spend it on. Bachelors returning from their high-roller vacations always had great stories to share with their buddies—or if it was a bust, they invented even better ones.

# Timeline

| | |
|---|---|
| Born at the Salvation Army Home for Unwed Mothers, Spokane, WA | June 21, 1937 |
| Start work at MIT Lincoln Laboratory, Lexington, MA | Spring, 1961 |
| Daughter #1 born, Boston, MA | Oct., 1961 |
| Began first tour on Kwajalein | Fall 1963 |
| Daughter #2 born, Kwajalein | May, 1964 |
| End first tour (return to MIT graduate school in fall) | Spring, 1965 |
| Daughter #3 born, Boston, MA | Oct., 1965 |
| Began second tour on Kwajalein | Spring, 1966 |
| End second tour. Divorce. Began U of Colorado grad school, Boulder; single father with daughters, ages 2, 3, and 6 | Fall, 1968 |
| Begin third tour on Kwajalein | Fall, 1970 |
| End final Kwajalein tour | Spring, 1972 |
| Chase girlfriend to Palo Alto, marry, have daughters #4, #5, still here | Fall, 1977 |

# 1

# SHARKS, SHIPS, AND SHELLS

"Pete, damn! Sorry to screw up your photo. That great white really got my heart pumping! So exciting. Didn't mean to spook him. Couldn't hold back."

"That's OK—could happen to anybody. Might get another chance. Yikes, it sure was big though, wasn't it?"

"Wow! I know they get a lot bigger, but that was, without doubt, the biggest great white shark I've ever seen—much less been in the water with. Damn, it was big! Looked like a ten-footer. Felt like a 100-footer. OK, I exaggerate. Goggles made him seem a lot bigger. He was probably more like seven or eight. Actually, the more excited I get, the bigger the shark gets. I was so caught up, I totally forgot my number one diving rule."

"Oh? And what rule is that?" Pete queried.

"When there is something in the water bigger than me, *I get out!*"

"Good rule."

Four of us—Royce, Larry, Pete, and I—had invested three and a half very bumpy and spray-ridden hours that Saturday morning in a small Boston whaler (fifteen-foot skiff) transiting the entire lagoon to reach Ebadon, the most remote corner of the Kwajalein Atoll (the largest of the Marshall Island's twenty-nine atolls). Our cargo consisted of our diving gear, lunches, and the three extra tanks of gas needed to make such a long voyage. We lived on Kwajalein Island (Kwaj) at the southern tip of the banana-shaped atoll, worked on Roi-Namur (Roi), at the northeastern tip, and were now diving seventy miles from Kwaj and forty miles from Roi at Ebadon on the northwestern tip of the atoll. Ebadon, the third-largest island of the atoll, had been virtually abandoned by the Marshallese for years, though it had been an important Marshallese village prior to World War II. During the time of our exploration trip in the late 1960s, it was probably visited no more than a couple times a year for coconut harvesting (dried to make copra, a source of coconut oil and a major Marshallese export) and for performing special ancestral rites. Of the ninety-six islands or so in the entire Kwajalein Atoll, none were more remote nor more untouched—which of course enticed us all the more. It was virgin territory—not picked over by the Kwajalein snorkelers and shell-hunters like the closer and more accessible diving areas.

After we donned our scuba gear and plunged in, Pete and I headed east while Royce and Larry headed west to ensure that we would not run into each other. We were immediately rewarded for our efforts by the sight of beautiful, undisturbed coral formations and a plethora of colorful fish. Other than this incredible display, the dive was relatively uneventful for the first half hour.

But then, suddenly, our tranquil environment was disturbed by an unwelcoming committee of one—the largest great white (GW) shark I had ever encountered in my many years of diving experience—who decided to investigate the odd creatures who had invaded his neighborhood. Although exciting, this first visit also proved to be a bit of a disappointment, for he lingered no more than thirty seconds before he lost interest and poof, vanished.

My disappointment stemmed from my failure to be camera-ready. I had loaded a fresh roll of film into my underwater camera just before entering the water but was so gaga to see Mr. GW that I forgot to take any pictures.

This letdown proved to be a fleeting setback, however, as five minutes later, GW paid us a second visit. (The thought did briefly pass through my mind that perhaps his short absence was to scurry off and let his big brothers know that dinner was ready.)

Ah, but this time I was ready. As he approached for this second go-around, I was able to get off six shots before he disappeared again. I knew these photos would be sketchy at best, as I had taken them from a distance of forty feet and Mr. GW chose not to pose for long. Pete had a similar experience and only managed to snap four during our second "encounter of the GW kind."

Twenty minutes later and running low on air, we began to work our way back toward the boat, still a good 300 yards to our west. That's when our friend, GW, decided that a third foray to investigate us in more detail was warranted. Frustrated by my lack of good shots during our first two encounters and guessing from his lackluster behavior that there would unlikely be a fourth visit, I tried to squeeze in as many pictures as I could, moving in closer and closer with each shot. With two pictures left, the desire to make them my best shots clouded my judgment; I inadvertently became too aggressive. When I was about eight feet away, GW decided he had had enough and took off in a huff (or a shark's equivalent of a huff). That's when I knew I had spoiled it for Pete.

Five minutes later, with a virtual vacuum in our scuba tanks, we reached the boat and clambered aboard. We were puzzled—both Pete and I could stretch out our air supply far longer than even the most experienced divers (we could ration our air consumption to four to five breaths a minute), so Larry and Royce should already have been waiting for us in the boat upon our return. When the wind finally took a temporary lull, we heard and then saw our two missing diving companions yelling and waving their arms, beseeching our attention from shore. We pulled anchor and headed in to fetch them.

"Did you see that great white? He kept making closer and closer passes at us! We decided we had better head for shore—it was closer than the boat. We hoped the shallow water would discourage him from attacking us."

These seasoned divers were absolutely convinced that they had been within seconds of an attack by our shared great white.

So while we were unintentionally scaring away GW, he was scaring away our friends. Why the difference?

It was a matter of posture. Anxious to get good pictures, we became the aggressors, and GW decided to have nothing to do with us—particularly as he found a more timid alternative a few hundred feet past three large coral heads. The other two divers retreated from GW each time he edged further into their comfort zone. Their timidity made them appear to be the weaker, and thus the safer, prey. When not checking on us, he made closer and closer passes at them, taking measure of these potential morsels, testing their responses, and planning his next move. Contrary to Hollywood lore, unless they are whipped into a frenzy, sharks tend to be very cautious until they are convinced that the potential reward warrants more assertive probing. This is taught as "risk analysis" in business schools. Sharks tend to be risk averse, which is probably why they have been such successful survivors for the last 400-million years.

## MY CONCLUSION

My conclusion was to always dive with an underwater camera. It is the closest thing there is to an effective shark repellant. Some divers claim that having a camera loaded and ready automatically makes them more aggressive than the shark cares to deal with. Actually I think the real reason is that sharks, like some people, do not like their picture taken. Oh—and never run out of film (no longer a problem with digital cameras). For some reason, sharks always seem to know when you have just taken your last picture.

One diving friend tells me he always carries a knife when diving in shark waters.

"Is that so you can stab the shark if he gets too close?"

"Are you kidding? A diving knife won't even tickle a shark. No, no! If a shark ever gets too aggressive with me, I'll just poke my diving buddy with my knife to make him bleed, then swim like hell."

I had always wondered why this particular friend had difficulty finding diving buddies. Perhaps it was because no one was 100 percent sure he was kidding.

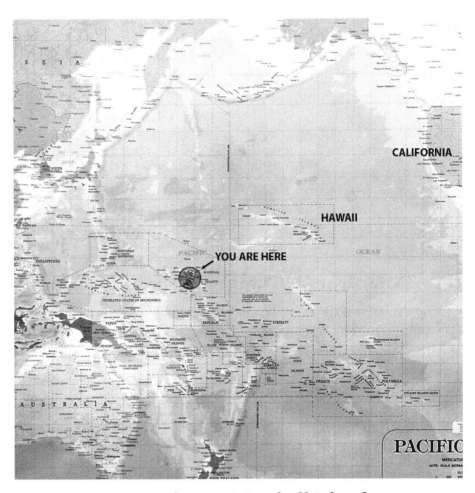

**You are here--Marshall Islands**

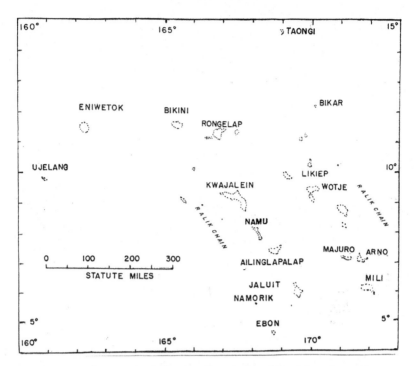

## Kwajalein Atoll in the Marshall Islands

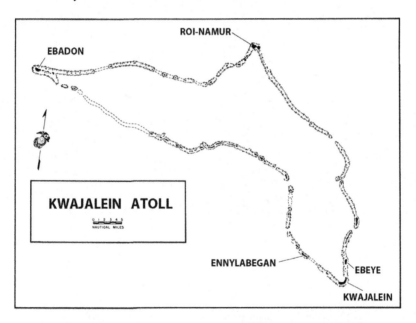

## Kwajalein Island in the Kwajalein Atoll

# 2

# BACK TO KWAJ

## (Kwaja-Lynn?)

### FIRST PIXEL

Whether a return from a home-base meeting in Boston, the end of a vacation, or the start of a new tour, I always preferred to settle into a window seat to endure the long, eleven-hour, nonstop military prop-plane flight from Hawaii to Kwajalein. For all but the last twelve minutes, the view mimicked an endless tape looping through indiscernible images of clouds and the seemingly infinite Pacific. However, this monotonous journey never dulled my excitement once the first pixel of *The Isle* floated on the horizon. My ninth such flight, to begin my third and final eighteen-month tour in the fall of 1970, was no different—except that it was to be my first tour as a bachelor.

My first eighteen-month tour began in the fall of 1963 shortly after I turned twenty-six. I was motivated to accept this opportunity by the allure of adventure, the chance to do state-of-the-art engineering research on a new program, and exceptional financial benefits while living on a tropical island in the middle of the Pacific, 2,450 miles west of Honolulu and nine degrees north of the equator. On that tour I arrived on Kwajalein with school debt, zero savings, a wife, and a two-year-old daughter. I finished that tour with no debt, a modest nest egg, a wife, and two daughters, plus an enhanced technical reputation. (I was told I did exceptional work, and I don't recall bribing anyone for their opinion.)

When MIT Lincoln Laboratory issued a request in mid-1966 for volunteers to re-up for an additional tour at their Kwajalein test site, (second in my case), the general responses of the Kwajalein veterans were as follows:

"You'll never get me back there!"

"Me neither."

"No way—once was more than enough."

"The wife would never stand for it."

Virtually all of my friends who had previously been on a Kwaj tour (Kwaj-ites) expressed a total lack of interest in, if not outright disdain for repeating the experience—at least when they were in a group.

I had had a different reaction.

"What problem?" I thought. "No taxes, thirty percent bonus, free housing, and inexpensive help with our now three highly energized, preschool-aged daughters. A second tour sounds good to me!"

So rather than join the chorus, I seized the next opportunity I had to meet with the powers that be and signed up for a second tour. Their guarantee that we would be assigned a house (albeit with only two bedrooms) rather than the trailer we endured during our first tour helped convince us this was a prudent decision.

Over the next few weeks, whenever I ran into two or more Kwaj-ites in the hall, they would barrage me with irritating questions.

"Why on earth would you want a second tour?"

"Don't you think life is so much better here?"

"You know it will ruin your career advancement. You won't have anyone looking out for your interests when you get back."

"You'll be on your own."

"The schools just aren't good enough."

Yet, when I would encounter a Kwaj-ite one-on-one, away from the influence of *groupthink*, his demeanor softened as well as his questions.

"Was it hard to re-up?"

"Do they still have openings?"

"Aren't you worried going back will hamper your career?"

Ultimately several of my adamant "No-wayer" Kwaj-ite friends joined me for a second tour.

Our second tour (fall of 1966 to the spring of 1968) held the promise of a less stressful environment than what we had living in Boston. In essence, it became an attempt to save a marriage or, if that failed, to at least allow us to accumulate sufficient funds for both of us to move on. More graduate school, a third degree, intensive work, and a third daughter complicated the ramifications of adjusting to family life for two young, overbooked, inexperienced parents with different expectations. We both felt a second tour would help ease this overwhelming family pressure if not actually resolve our conflicts.

As a veteran, I knew day-to-day life on Kwaj was far less demanding than in Boston. Housing was taken care of, utilities and entertainment were free, cars were not needed, and a minimum set of heavy clothing was only kept for short visits back home. Local television was at least eight years in the future, off-island phone service was unavailable, medical coverage was affordable and within walking distance, and the burden of day-to-day domestic maintenance (i.e., three daughters) was lightened with help from inexpensive Marshallese maids.

We gave it a go, but the effort didn't save the marriage.

Now in the fall of 1970, I was headed back to begin what was to be my third and final Kwaj tour. I hoped to financially recover from the expenses incurred during the previous two years as a divorced graduate-student father caring for three daughters under the age of nine. My goal was to replenish my coffers to the point where I could complete my PhD thesis and still have sufficient funds for the down payment on a house. I knew the Kwajalein opportunity and valuable perks would not last forever, so I quickly accepted MIT's generous solicitation and signed up for a third tour.

We landed.

I couldn't help but muse, "Am I starting my third tour on Kwajalein, or have I just finished my third tour in the States?"

# 3

# NEWBIES

Kwajalein is hot—I mean, really hot. At least it seems that way when flying directly there from New England. You land. The door opens. Pow! One hundred hair dryers aimed directly in your face make it clear: you're not in Boston anymore.

"He must be new."

"Why do you say that?"

"He's sweating. After a couple of weeks, we all adjust and stop sweating unless, of course, we are involved in a physical activity."

Newbies also spend all their time looking out the window when commuting by air to work (fifty miles north), whereas old-timers have their noses buried in large tomes. I personally read the entire six volumes of Winston Churchill's *History of World War II* during my first year, J.R.R. Tolkien's *Hobbit* and *Lord of the Rings* my second year, and every book I could find on South Pacific history after that.

## GETTING STARTED

Buy local attire/uniform including Bermuda shorts and Hawaiian shirts (visitors broadcast their status by wearing long pants). Island formal is defined as your best Bermuda shorts, newest Hawaiian shirt, and an upgrade to fancy sandals from flip-flops.

Buy cheap sandals (local names: go-gos, go-aheads; Japanese name: *zories*; American names: flip-flops, shower slippers—all the same thing). Explore entire nine-hundred-acre island on foot in new attire. Second week, switch back to shoes until the intrusive blisters between the big and second toes heal. Fourth week, develop calluses to allow switching back to go-aheads.

By fifth week, sunscreen use drops off (bad idea) as deceptively healthy-looking tans replace pale, washed-out skin.

By sixth week, residents adjust to the point where lunchtime activities include four-mile jogs under the noonday sun (so high it casts no shadows), volleyball, swimming, exploration of numerous jungle/beach war remnants, and diving on sunken ships.

Somewhere around three months, newbies start to understand what "having money to invest" means. They are now convinced that they will be able to save as much money in eighteen months as would normally take them ten years. Once they see the real dollars piling up in their bank accounts, they become true believers.

After spending six months on Kwaj, many families take their first vacation to Hawaii. By this time they have all become Kwaj-conditioned to believe that driving at twenty miles per hour was fast and twenty-five miles per hour was careening recklessly down the road. When they reached Hawaii, they found the first few minutes driving on the Hawaiian freeways absolutely terrifying.

At a year, a first trip back to Massachusetts (with its even more overwhelming traffic) dictates that the nearly forgotten warm clothes be retrieved from the back of the closet to protect the now-wimpy Kwajalein-adjusted residents against the hundred-degrees-below zero weather they will undoubtedly encounter.

## NEWBIE-GRADUATE'S WEEKDAY ROUTINE

The morning getting-ready-for-work rush, between waking and getting out the door, was pretty much the same on Kwajalein as it was stateside, except sandals replaced shoes, Bermuda shorts replaced long pants, and Hawaiian shirts replaced both under-shirts and dress shirts. Once out the door, the similarities ceased. I usually rode my bike the half mile to the airport (or walked during periods of heavy rain) where I would catch my 7:05 a.m. (9:30 a.m. if late) commute flight from Kwajalein, my island of residence, to Roi-Namur, my work island.

My briefcase held an umbrella to protect me against the ambushing rain squalls, a book I hoped to make headway on during the twenty-to-thirty minute flight, a snack in case I missed lunch, and a lesson plan for the course I was teaching in the evenings.

A bus picked us commuters up at the Roi terminal and dropped us off at the TRADEX building where I had my office. (During the 1960s, the TRADEX radar was the most advanced radar in the world).

My work routine during each of my three tours varied as my specialty progressed from digital interfaces to optics, and finally to operations.

At lunch I would swim a mile in the Roi pool, run four miles around the runway, take karate lessons, beach comb, play volleyball, explore the Japanese ruins, or wander through the seldom-visited jungle.

The bus picked us up at 5:05 p.m. where it had dropped us off and returned us to the Roi airport for our 5:15 p.m. flight back to Kwaj.

We had reentry missile missions typically three nights a month, during which I would remain on Roi well into the night.

Once I retrieved my bike at 5:45 p.m., I headed to Macy's (our local army PX) to see what may have newly arrived that day. I entered the store between 5:50 p.m. and 5:55 p.m. every weekday and recognized about twenty individuals who were leaving the store at the same time, although I never actually met any of them or ever learned their names.

Then it was home to my trailer during my first tour, my duplex during my second tour, or the BQ (bachelors' quarters) during my third tour.

My children, with me during my first two tours, would meet me at the door as soon as I arrived home and insist we head off for our half-hour predinner adventures—with up to six neighborhood kids joining in to keep it lively. Following dinner, my final hour or two would be spent reading to my daughters and putting them to sleep with a few off-key songs.

During my third, bachelor tour, I taught swimming five evenings a week (plus Saturday swim lessons) at 6:15 p.m. and taught college courses for the University of Hawaii two late evenings a week at 8:00 p.m. When not teaching I just hung out with friends, graded homework, read, and tried to learn the guitar.

# 4

# BACHELORS— THE 60 PERCENT

Bachelors made up 60 percent of the Kwajalein population in the 1960s, and families accounted for the remaining 40% percent. The vast majority of bachelors who worked on Kwajalein spent much of their working careers bouncing among the remote offshore US military installations (Kwajalein Atoll, Johnston Island, and Palmyra Atoll). They either extended their contracts contiguously or took a few months off between gigs. Some bachelors swore "Never again!" However, within six months most had a change of heart (i.e., ran out of money and still had no girlfriend) and signed up for "that one last tour."

During the 1960s and 1970s, the site's labor policies did not allow women on bachelorette status to participate in the onsite workforce. The misguided goal of this policy was supposedly to maintain stability in the Kwajalein living environment. From the bachelors' perspectives, enduring the lack of female companionship or even the lack of female presence for six to twelve months at a time only added to their hardships.

## TWO LEVELS

The more highly ranked bachelors took their meals at the Yokwe Yuk Club, which had previously been the officers' club. *Yokwe yuk* is the traditional Marshallese greeting not unlike aloha in Hawaiian and literally means "love to you." The worker bees had their own separate mess hall—equivalent to a noncommissioned officers' club. The higher-ranking and lower-ranking bachelors tended not to mix, primarily due to the reduced social interaction inherent in their housing and dining arrangements. Outside of this separation, I never personally observed any class-tainted friction between these two groups.

## Adoption

A subset of bachelors ultimately attached themselves to a family or two, enjoying the hospitality and warmth of a family environment. They contributed more than their share by arranging and paying for barbecues, parties, and diving excursions, and by providing good company. Some ultimately became part of the family—almost like an adoption. Many just remained friends, and still a few other relationships progressed to the point where they eventually ended up with the wife.

These mate-exchanges did not tend to last when the idyllic island conditions on Kwajalein met the harsh realities of off-island life head-on. Money and attention could be spent lavishly on a person of interest on Kwajalein, but life off island always became far more challenging. Reality set in. Differences in cultural backgrounds and interests, inherently on the back burner in the liberal but limited Kwajalein environment, surfaced once back home.

Budgets became squeezed as consumption ratcheted up considerably due to the additional demands of rent, auto expenses, insurance, entertainment, and higher taxes, while both opportunities and income fell off dramatically. All these factors created far more financial stress than anticipated and tested the "love is blind" concept.

It was common for new relationships forged on Kwajalein to reach their demise before their first anniversary.

## Keeping to Themselves

The Kwajalein Crossroads Bachelors Club (and the Jackaroo Bachelors Club for the *Roi Rats* on Roi-Namur) provided inexpensive drinks. (On the mainland, a barkeep diluted "rum and Cokes" by skimping on the rum and going heavy on the Coke to cut costs. On Kwaj, this cost-cutting bias was reversed by skimping on the

Coke and going heavy on the rum.) With free movies and good camaraderie, some bachelors preferred to stay apart from families altogether and pass their time socializing with work associates and friends. Others busied themselves with gambling, golf, skin diving, ham radio, sailing, flying lessons, other physical activities, or even expanding their education by taking night courses at the University of Hawaii, Kwajalein Extension (where I taught calculus).

## FRINGE STUFF

Severe gambling addictions, alcoholism, the pursuit of Marshallese girlfriends on Ebeye (including a few relationships that progressed to marriage), and zealous evangelistic pursuits were all part of the Kwaj mix. Needless to say, depression was a big problem, and a suicide would occur every year or two, usually as a result of *Dear John* letters, ill-advised investments, family problems, and health issues—all heightened by the island's isolation.

There were also the few inevitable ongoing romances between some of the youngest bachelors and some of the high school seniors and, of course, a few summer romances when college-aged daughters returned to Kwaj for their summer vacations.

# 5

# Bachelors On/Off Island

## CARL

Carl showed up in my office the first morning after his arrival on Kwajalein to begin a two-year contract as my lead technician.

The very first subject Carl brought up went like this:

"Lynn, I thought I should let you know upfront where I stand. During my last twenty years, I've had eight different contracts at three separate remote installations similar to this one. By now I know myself. The only reason I've been able to handle the long isolations is because I follow certain rules—rules that at least work for me.

"The first thing I do the moment I arrive at a new site is to spend a week searching for the ugliest woman, at least in my eyes, that I can find on the island. I nickname her Belle, short for my bellwether woman. After that, I faithfully check Belle out once every couple of weeks. When she starts looking good to me, I know I'm ready for a vacation so—if I come to you on short notice requesting leave, you will know why."

Carl proved to be one of the best technicians I worked with throughout my entire Kwajalein experience. I was very happy to have him on my team and trusted his judgment implicitly.

Seven months later.

"Lynn, not only does Belle look awfully good to me but Big Bob [the three-hundred-pound cook], is starting to look good too."

"Go—please go! For the safety of all of us, go! I'll see you in a couple of weeks."

## FRANK

Although less educated than most of the technical personnel on island, Frank was a very likeable and hard-working assistant engineer who barely made the cut when it came to qualifying for family housing.

Frank, his wife Sara, and their eleven-year-old daughter occupied the other half of our duplex, so we could not help but be somewhat aware of their day-to-day activities. I would classify Frank as a loving and caring husband, though their relatively mild arguments that penetrated our shared wall told me that his understanding of women and knowledge of what it took to achieve marital bliss were limited.

Sara was a pleasant but rather ordinary and somewhat boring woman. Frankly, Mother Nature had not been generous when allocating her share of natural beauty and intellect and perhaps too generous in allocating her share of bulk. It is probable that her extra poundage and underachievement in fashion were major contributors to her general demeanor.

Shortly after their arrival on Kwajalein, a bachelor fireman attached himself to the family, which, as described previously, was not unusual. He had not been off island for nearly a year (way past the seven-month danger point) and did not have Carl's self-awareness, so Sara looked like a very attractive option to him, and quite probably she signaled that she was "available." In short order, she left Frank and her daughter and ran off to Hawaii with her new love, anticipating a newfound life of pure happiness.

Within a few weeks of their arrival in Hawaii, the fireman's concept of what constituted a woman's beauty went through serious recalibration, and he dumped her. The rest of the story is unknown, as Frank and his daughter left Kwaj soon afterward. Rumor had it that he eventually took Sara back—at least that's what I'd like to think happened. (Actually I was happy to see them leave for the sake of their eleven-year-old daughter's safety, as she was starting to behave very flirtatiously with the bachelors—her way of getting attention.)

I concluded that the fireman's actions were motivated by Mother Nature's Rule Number One—"More babies equals survival." But what motivated Sara? That's easy. Many women thrive on attention, and the fireman was providing her with this valuable commodity in far greater abundance than her husband did. But there is more to the story than that.

Kwajalein heavily skewed relationship dynamics. Bachelors, normally struggling to meet their financial obligations, benefited from both higher incomes and the lack of anything to spend them on and became more self-assured. So a lavish standard of living was assumed and provided a foundation to woo with confidence— a bubble destined to burst soon after returning home to reality.

## TOM

Tom was a very talented bachelor engineer and a good friend. During my last tour, the two of us spent many evenings hanging out and solving the world's problems. As Tom was on his first tour and I on my third, I felt obliged to give him the following old-timer advice:

"Tom, what you don't understand is that as a bachelor, your bonus is not based on your extra hours of work, but is instead, compensation for a lack of female companionship. In essence, it's a form of negative prostitution. The longer you are here, the more your mind wanders to the fantasy of spending the night with the beautiful and affectionate woman of your dreams. If you divide your monthly bonus by the number of times you think about being with her, it works out to be about two hundred dollars per time, on the order of a woman of the night's fee."

"Oh my God, you're right. I never thought of it that way before."

That was during his second month on site. At month six, he came to me with: "I've been thinking about what you said—it's now down to twenty-five dollars per fantasy."

He took a vacation the next week and met his girlfriend in Maui. Hopefully, neither he nor his girlfriend, whom he eventually married, will ever read this book.

# 6

# BACHELOR MANNY

## (Love at First Site)

"I don' need to take your sh** no more! Always at me, always on me back. Never give me no respect. Me no tak'n it no more!"

With this not uncertain declaration, Manny took a swing at his boss. Fortunately he missed his intended target.

"I quit!"

"Pack up—you're outta here!"

When not in Honolulu staying with his extended family and working odd jobs, Manny worked at remote military installation sites all over the Pacific as a carpenter. His last and longest such tour landed him on Roi-Namur (the northeastern tip of the Kwajalein atoll). He was a mediocre carpenter at best who suffered from a Napoleon complex due to his five-foot-six stature, his limited ninth-grade education, and his poor track record with girls.

His life had taken a turn for the better six years earlier when he met Liana, the first and only love of his life. She was a petite, pretty, high-energy, and affectionate local girl whom he had met on one of his annual four-week home leaves. He had been attending a local Hawaiian open-air concert when she spilled a Coke on him while working her way through the crowd. She apologized profusely and used her napkins to wipe up the mess she had made as best she could—he only saw her. They talked. She stayed with him, never making it back to her friends waiting for their drinks.

By the end of his stay, they were fully committed if not actually engaged. They made extensive plans that included marriage, children, and saving for a house, which he would build. They figured four to five more years of his working and saving on Kwajalein would give them enough of a nest egg to make their dreams come true.

"I no good with money or saving," he admitted. "Numbers just confuse me—but give me a hammer and I know what to do."

"That OK. I work as a bookkeeper so I really good at that. No worry. I take care of that for both of us. I put what I can in our joint account and you do the same. I live with Momma so can save more now that I have a reason. We will do good with our savings."

It was agreed. They opened a joint savings account to save for the day they would begin to live out their dreams together. Every month he would automatically deposit most of his paycheck into their account, keeping out just enough for his modest immediate living expenses and of course for their annual month of bliss together in Hawaii. She would do the same, but less of course, as she had less income and higher expenses.

"I know I make littler than you but I spend very little. Maybe save half. It's not much but more better if I do my share."

During their month together each year, they reaffirmed their commitment to each other, planned how many kids they wanted, gave them all names, and designed their perfect home. They had playful spats arguing over the color of their bedroom and what make of pickup truck he should buy when he returned.

She never introduced him to any of her family or her friends, claiming she wanted to keep him all to herself during his too-short visits, implying that her parents would not approve of her seeing someone with so little education.

"I introduce you to them when time is good. In meantime, I tell them how nice you are and most important, how good you are to me. They like that a lot 'cause they think my last boyfriend mean to me and not nice to them at all. I know they will like you, and Momma want grandkids more than anything."

Six years had passed since they first met. He figured this had to be plenty of time to have saved enough to begin their life together. Granted they lost a year when her mother had an accident, and Liana had to dip into their account to see her through. Liana assured him: "Momma, she promised me she pay it all back in year or two when she get the insurance money from the accident," so he figured this setback was temporary.

Manny's last trip back to Hawaii, a few months before, did not go quite as smoothly as their previous rendezvous, which made him a bit nervous. "Yes," he decided, "Time to stop planning. Time to start living." He was so emboldened by the thought of starting his new life with Liana that he had no reservations about taking a swing at his hated nemesis.

"I don't need this f***ing job no more. I'm set, so you can take this job and shove it!"

He left on the next flight back to Honolulu. Carl, my technician, was one of his friends who saw Manny off and kept me updated as to what was happening in his life.

Two weeks later Carl received a letter from Manny, or rather, The Letter. It began something like this:

"Dear Carl, could you please borrow me $500 until I find job? I real broke right now and owe lotta money on my credit card. Also could you talk to my old boss tell him how sorry I am. Ask him if I can get my old job back?"

To Carl's credit, he sent the five hundred dollars without hesitation, knowing it was unlikely he would ever see any of it again.

Manny's second letter a few weeks later thanked Carl for the loan and shed more light on his predicament. In essence, his unexpected return on such short notice caught Liana off guard. When he told her he had quit his job so that now they were free to pursue their plans with the money they had saved, she did not react as he expected. Instead, she informed him that after considerable soul searching, she had come to the conclusion that they had drifted too far apart and should call things off. "I like you lot, but it's just not love no more. I wanta go back to school and need be by myself, live with my family."

Manny was devastated—six years of planning, dreaming, and fantasizing—poof, all up in smoke.

"What about all the money I send you—six years I send you all my money. How much we now have?"

"I loan some to my brother who promised to pay it back in few months but he go to Las Vegas and I no hear from him. Then I lose my job almost year ago so needed rest to get by on. I sure I find job right 'way, but didn't. Too scared to tell you. Don't want you angry. Don't want you worry. Just kept hopin' somethin' good happen, make it all OK. No money left. All gone. Credit cards all full. If my brother pay me back loan, I send it to you."

A few months later Carl received a third letter from Manny in which he elaborated on his plight in more detail. After checking around a bit over the next few months, Manny figured out the whole operation. For the past eight years, Liana had averaged between two and five "fiancés" at any one time, all of whom were sending earnings to "joint accounts" from overseas sites to build up savings for their dream life together. She would juggle their vacation times so no two were in town at the same time and made sure they never met her family or any of her friends. She selected the lonely, the insecure, and those with low self-esteem as her prey. It was easy. With her beauty, her ability to feign warmth and interest, her charm, intimacy, and attention, she had no problem keeping and upgrading her collection of lonely hearts as opportunities arose. Her biggest two problems were to ensure that no two victims worked at the same site, or if they did, they knew her by separate aliases, and to make sure that she could control their leave schedules.

It's what Liana did for a living.

"My biggest hurt," concluded Manny, "is now I think—the spilt Coke was no accident. She plan it all 'long."

No one ever heard from Manny again after his third letter.

# 7

# BACHELOR BOB AND BACHELOR CHARLIE

## BOB

Bob was the opposite of Manny. Whereas Manny was small statured, uneducated, and relatively young, naive, and unsure of himself, Bob was six foot one, a widowed former college professor, sophisticated, a few months away from a double-dip retirement, and as head of security for our Kwajalein operation, very confident.

Bob came to Kwajalein for a double three-year tour where the money was good and expenses low to save that last extra nest egg to guarantee him a more comfortable retirement. He planned on retiring to Hawaii once this final tour was over and was comfortable with the thought of living out his remaining years in Paradise.

New environments can create new opportunities, and Hawaii has a stronger impact in this way than almost anywhere else. Bob, with no expectations, did meet someone on his last preretirement leave to Hawaii—someone who revitalized his sense of youth and thirst for life. He discovered that eligible bachelors were in great demand in Hawaii regardless of age—especially if they had solid financial resources.

The upshot of his next twelve months was he retired, moved to Hawaii, married a few months later, bought a condo and two fancy cars, and seemed quite happy to mutual friends who looked him up while passing through Hawaii. Then surprise, surprise—he turned up back on Kwajalein.

My only firsthand information after his return was when I overheard him say to a colleague, "She took me for nearly everything I had."

It appears Manny and Bob were not so different after all.

## CHARLIE

My nickname for Charlie was Coconut Head. Charlie, one of my better technicians, was sixty-two, easygoing, likable, and always seemed to do things in either twos or threes.

Charlie was standing beneath a coconut tree on Roi-Namur holding a beer in one hand and a hamburger in the other, enjoying one of the Roi-Rat luaus his colleagues put on every weekend.

Then, *pow!* A coconut fell from the tree he was leaning against and grazed his left temple. He was knocked down, but other than being embarrassed and spilling most of his beer, was not seriously hurt.

"Charlie. Move away from that tree. It's too dangerous." So he moved to the other side of the party and leaned against another coconut tree.

*Pow!* A coconut fell and grazed his other temple. I have personally never known anyone else who has been hit by a falling coconut, much less by two within ten minutes. After that his friends limited him to only small beers. "Charlie, if you are going to keep letting coconuts knock you down, we can't let you waste all that beer."

This trend paralleled his love life as well—Charlie had had three tours on Kwajalein, each following one of his three divorces, all from the same woman. I am convinced there is a third coconut out there somewhere with his name on it just waiting to finish the job.

There were several successful marriages between returning bachelors and women they met while on Kwajalein, so not all had unhappy endings. In fact, one good friend married the boss's daughter while on island, and they were quite happy the last time I heard from them fifteen years later.

# 8

# DOES NOT COMPUTE

"Gotta be exaggerating." I was sure of it. "No tree could be that big. Impossible. No way." My older eight-year-old brother had just returned from his first month-long summer camp experience in northern Minnesota and described with great enthusiasm his hike with fellow campers deep into the woods. Their quest was to reach the largest pine tree in the whole of Minnesota.

"Five of us with arms stretched out like this couldn't even reach all the way 'round it!" he enthused. This flagrant exaggeration was beyond even my own inflated imagination. It just couldn't be. I tried to envision even three eight-year-olds not being able to embrace what had to be the largest tree in the world. (I was positive Minnesota was at least 95 percent of the known world at that time.)

"No way."

Three years later, shortly after my own eighth birthday, I attended this same camp and hiked to this very same tree. I was surprised to discover that he had spoken the truth. The stretched-out arms of five eight-year-olds trying to encircle the tree still left a two-foot gap.

Ninety percent of the US population (ninety-nine percent if they grew up in Minnesota) would react to a description of a Pacific atoll as I had reacted to the description of the aforementioned giant tree. "No way." It is just too far beyond their realm of personal experience to accept—too unbelievable.

"Let me get this straight. After you leave Honolulu and cross over nearly 2,500 miles of three-mile-deep open ocean, you reach a ring of one hundred or so islands, encircling a body of water forty to seventy miles across but not even two hundred feet deep. Yeah.

Right. Tell you what—if you let me smoke some of what you've been smoking, I'll make a really big effort to believe you."

The concept of a few high mountaintops in the middle of the Pacific poking through the surface is acceptable, but a hundred low (average elevation six feet above sea level) islands aligned in the shape of a distorted banana enclosing a very large, shallow lagoon, makes no sense.

Explain to someone unfamiliar with marine geology, "If you head twenty miles toward the middle of the lagoon, the water will be between one hundred and two hundred feet deep. However, if you head ten miles in the opposite direction, into the open ocean, it could easily be a mile deep." They might smile politely but would firmly believe that, as Robbie the Robot once said, "It does not compute." Among the reasons supporting their disbelief would be an internal dialogue: Six feet above sea level—one big storm and the whole place would disappear. And I'd hate to think what would happen if a tsunami came along—it would all go *poof!*; or, So what are you going to tell me next? Aliens filled in the big hole in the middle of the lagoon with sand brought from Mars?

Atolls are the remains of a fringing reef formerly surrounding a mountain—long since eroded, leaving only a ring of islands enclosing a lagoon. (See chapter 12 for more details.)

On our first vacation back from Kwajalein to visit my parents at their Minnesota lakefront home, D1 (daughter one) ran down to the lakeshore all excited and called back, "Daddy, Daddy, is this the ocean side or the lagoon side? And look, you can see all the way across it!" It's all about what we're used to, isn't it?

When Allison, aged eleven, one of my favorite Kwaj swim students, returned home to Boston after an eighteen-month hiatus, she immediately sought out her old friends in the neighborhood and reveled in the renewal of old ties. Nonstop talk, talk, talk. After a few minutes of describing to her friends her strange experience of living on a tiny island in such an exotic and remote place with five thousand people, the subject somehow petered out. Her friends couldn't bring up images to interpret the descriptions they were being fed. It was beyond their personal range of reality and therefore soon held little interest for them—there was no way they could contribute to the conversation.

"Daddy, they haven't been anywhere!" she explained to her father when she came in for dinner. The subject of her Kwajalein experiences never arose again except within her family or when other Kwaj-ites dropped by to visit.

# 9

# KWAJALEIN, KWAJALEIN

Just as New York is both the name of a city and the state in which it is located, Kwajalein is both the name of the largest island (22 percent of total atoll landmass) and of the atoll—so like New York, New York, there is Kwajalein, Kwajalein.

The entire 840-square-mile atoll of four-thousand-plus acres of land is comprised of ninety-seven islands, plus or minus a couple depending on one's definition of an island, arranged in a distorted circular configuration. Its outline is perhaps best described as a seventy-five-mile-long banana when viewed from a satellite. The US government leases eleven of these islands, mostly at the atoll's southern tip, from the Marshallese.

Ownership of all Micronesia, including the Marshall Islands, was ceded to Spain by Portugal as part the 1494 Treaty of Tordesillas, brokered by Pope Alexander VI to clarify land ownership claims in the New World. The Marshall Islands were not actually discovered until 1529, when the Spaniard Alvaro Saavedra spotted them while seeking a western route to the "Spice Islands." They were given their current name in 1788 by British Naval Captain William Marshall when he passed through the region transporting convicts to New South Wales.

Although the Reverend Hiram Bingham Jr. provided America with the first (albeit minor) presence in this area by founding a Mormon mission outpost on Ebon in 1857, it was a German, Adolph Capelle, who initiated the first true development. In the 1860s he built the first large-scale trading company and thus brought commercial interest to these islands. Under the mediation of Pope Leo XIII in 1885, the German government annexed the Marshall Islands with \$4.5 million compensation paid to Spain and established a protectorate over them in 1886. Later, as a result of the Spanish-American war, Germany added Ujelang and Enewetak in 1898.

There had been a long history of interisland conflicts, including bloody battles among the various Marshallese clans, up until Germany assumed administration of the region, after which hostilities diminished considerably.

Following Germany's 1918 defeat in World War I, the Japanese outmaneuvered the Chinese to take over administration of the Marshall Islands (officially sanctioned by a League of Nations mandate in 1920) and slowly but peacefully began to develop them.

As World War II approached, Japan's intentions for the islands' future morphed from that of a benign civil administration into that of a harsh military dictatorship. They proceeded to build bases on the larger islands (Mili, Jaluit, Maloelap, Wotje, and Kwajalein) as rapidly as possible to protect their North Pacific flank from the United States. Japan withdrew from the League of Nations in 1934 and in 1935, declared the Marshall Islands an integral part of the Japanese empire. They brought in Korean conscripted laborers during the late 1930s and early 1940s to build a 6,700-foot runway on Kwajalein (in place of the Marshallese school) and to construct additional fortifications. In the process, the Japanese relocated their civil administration headquarters south to Namu Atoll and forcibly dispersed the Kwajalein Marshallese to many of the "less strategic" islands.

After World War II, the North Pacific area, which included the Marshall Islands, was reorganized as the UN-sanctioned six-district US Trust Territory (one of the districts being the Marshall Islands) to be administered by the US government until the region could establish self-rule. Total devastation from the US invasion finalized the depletion of Marshallese from Kwajalein Island. All that remained after four days of fighting were several thousand US troops, 206 Japanese prisoners of war out of nearly 5,000 defenders, and one lone palm tree (still there in 1972 when I departed).

The US government then leased eleven of the ninety-six islands from the Marshallese to carry out their post–World War II mandates, which included support for the Bikini and Eniwetok nuclear weapons testing as well as for ongoing Asian conflicts.

The amount of actual US payments to the Marshallese credited toward the Kwajalein lease payment is a little difficult to determine but seems to have been in the ten to fifteen million-dollar range.

Following World War II, the US Navy maintained the administration of Kwajalein operations. In the early 1960s, the mission of the facilities was redirected to support the newly established Kwajalein missile-reentry research facility. At that time, the navy felt the Kwajalein operations were no longer aligned with their naval military mandate, so they lobbied for an alternate command to be established. As a result, command was transferred to the army, consolidating missile launch communications and the corresponding reentry test program under a single branch of the military.

During the ceremony to transfer control, workers quickly replaced all naval signage with army signage. Ten minutes after the conclusion of the formal ceremony, the large eight-foot anchor symbolizing navy command was removed without ceremony from the front of the airport terminal and plunked down in a remote part of the small boat marina. An hour later, a newly arrived visitor would have had no hint that the navy had ever been in charge.

During the 1960s and 1970s, only three of the eleven leased islands were occupied by US personnel supporting missile-reentry physics, while the eight nonoccupied islands were used primarily to house remote sensors and communication equipment.

## KWAJALEIN ISLAND (KWAJALEIN, KWAJALEIN)

Kwajalein Island, home to most of the five thousand expatriates in the late 1960s and the largest island in the atoll, has an area between eight hundred to nine hundred acres, including landfill dredged up from coral to accommodate additional housing, research facilities, and the antiballistic-missile launch pads. The facilities on Kwajalein Island were primarily devoted to "missile-defense" research and testing.

**Kwajalein Island**

**Roi-Namur Island**

## ROI-NAMUR

Roi-Namur, the second-largest island in the atoll, with about four hundred acres, was "relandscaped" in the late 1930s when the Japanese bulldozed Roi, Namur, and two one-acre islets together as part of their fortification preparedness.

In the 1960s and early 1970s, approximately two hundred bachelor-status personnel were housed on Roi-Namur in dorm-like quarters in support of the army's reentry studies program. Roi was home to three state-of-the-art radars (it was said that TRADEX, the primary radar, could not only find a silver dollar in orbit but could tell you whether it was heads or tails), a 48-inch slewing telescope, a personnel housing/mess community, and several support structures. These all shared the island's real estate with an island-dividing 4,500-foot runway, a water catchment basin, and a jungle aggressively probing for the slightest opportunity to reclaim the entire island. The higher-level personnel (typically GS-11 equivalent and above) commuted the forty-five air miles between Kwaj and Roi each workday, and a few Marshallese commuted by small ferry from Enniburr, third island to the south on the east side, to provide support labor.

The facilities on Roi-Namur were devoted exclusively to "radar and sensing technology."

**Ebeye Island**

## EBEYE

Marshallese working on Kwajalein resided on Ebeye, the eighty-acre support island three miles to the northeast. In 1964 the Ebeye residents working on Kwaj began commuting to Kwaj via the ferry, *Tarlang*, ("Stormproof" in Marshallese), a converted LCU (Landing Craft Utility). *Tarlang* was eventually sold and replaced in 2008 by two high-speed ferries.

During the lowest ebb tides, it was said that one could negotiate the reef connecting Ebeye and Kwajalein (with two sub-acre islands, Little Bustard and Big Bustard, en route) by foot. Folklore had it that a few individuals, some of whom feared they would miss the last ferry, had successfully traversed this transit. Not a good idea, however, as there were also rumors claiming that at least one unlucky soul disappeared in his attempt.

**Typical Kwajalein Atoll islet**

## OTHER SUPPORT ISLANDS

Other islands that supported the Kwajalein operations were Ennylabegan, ninety acres, a few miles to the northwest, reachable by a small shuttle boat, and Meck, one hundred acres, a few miles to the northeast beyond Ebeye, serviced by a short takeoff-landing air shuttle. Meck was considered the island with the highest security level and as such was the most difficult to visit.

My favorite island names were Gugeegue and Bokenlabadoka, although Ailinglaplap Atoll was a close third.

The Japanese made several major alterations to the atoll's structure during their occupation and World War II defense preparations. In addition to creating the combined Roi-Namur Island, they blasted a shipping channel in the reef's northwest rim that shortened the supply route to Roi-Namur and built a large cement apron on Ebeye as part of their seaplane-base expansion.

# 10

# OPTICALLY CHALLENGED DIVING

Mark motioned to me again, this time even more animated than before. "OK," I thought, "I'll take one last look, but I have no idea what he expects me to see."

I swam down to where he was pointing once again, but this time, to account for my nearsightedness, I scanned the area much more closely, from twelve inches away instead of from three feet, and did a more methodical investigation. I very carefully inspected what seemed to be a smooth patch of gray coral but did not see anything out of the ordinary. At forty feet, the reds and blues are greatly attenuated compared to the greens, so to compensate, the brain interprets almost everything as gray. Information normally carried by the color differentiation is lost. As a result, objects are more difficult to identify.

"Nope. Nothing here."

I looked back toward Mark. He was getting even more agitated, and I had to conclude that our underwater hand signals were not working. Although I hated to make the extra effort, I swam to the surface to clarify what he was trying to tell me.

I broke the surface just after he did, removed my mask, and pulled out my mouthpiece, but before I could ask what his problem was, he blurted out, "You are either very brave or very blind."

"What do you mean?"

"Take another look at what's just under us."

I replaced my mask and looked straight down.

"Oh."

Directly beneath us was a seven-foot nurse shark, whose silhouette was quite clear against the lighter sand when viewed from above. I would have loved to take credit for being a macho diver, but I couldn't bluff—he knew me too well. It's the "can't see the forest for the trees" thing, but in this case I "couldn't see the shark for the sharkskin."

That is when I decided it might be prudent to order a set of prescription goggles that I had seen advertised in my latest skin-diving magazine.

The first time I tried them six weeks later, I discovered an amazing phenomenon. In my pre-prescription days, I could make out objects underwater up to about fifteen feet. Beyond that it was all a blur. I was convinced that without a doubt, ten-foot sharks all knew my visual limitation and would gather by the hundreds sixteen feet away from me—just beyond my ability to see them—waiting for their chance to dine.

With my new goggles, my improved vision extended to eighty feet. Now these same hundred or so hungry sharks moved back to an eighty-one-foot radius. I knew they were still there. I always felt their presence, but I never could understand how they were able to adjust so quickly to my new vision limits.

# 11

# SHELLS, SHARKS, AND SHIPS

## Killer Clam

### (*Tridacna gigas*)

This time it was Felix's turn to point out my underwater myopic handicap.

On this particular day, Felix, Royce, and I skipped the sunken cargo ship to explore a coral head two miles south of the Roi-Namur marina that Royce had spotted from the air that morning while flying to work from Kwaj. No one had ever mentioned this area as a location of interest, but we figured it was worth at least one exploration dive.

Fifteen minutes into our dive, Felix began making lively gestures toward a small patch on the lagoon floor just to our left in sixty feet of water. I moved in closer to see what all the fuss was about. All I saw was a very dark surface area about two and a half by three feet with a weak, florescent blue pattern. Felix, via hand signals, continued to indicate that this was something of great interest. I was studying the pattern from only six inches away and still could not identify what he was so excited about. Felix, in his frustration, finally signaled me to surface.

"You do realize you had your head in the bowels of a giant killer clam, don't you? I was just hoping I wouldn't run out of film before getting a couple of good shots of your newsworthy demise. The downside is you'd be dead—but the upside is I'd be famous!"

"Well, no. I was not aware of the seriousness of my predicament. Thank you very much."

"You're welcome. I was just worried that it might be difficult to get back to shore with a three-hundred-pound killer clam clamped over your head."

Once again, a repeat of not spotting the shark directly in front of me—this time it was a killer clam.

We dove back down to find that Felix was only half right—there were actually two killer clams about twelve feet apart. They were completely open—a totally new sight for me. I had never before seen one in that flat state, even in photos. In the past I had observed these clams open to 20 degrees or less and never imagined they could open up to a full 180 degrees. Usually I saw clams no longer than fifteen inches in length that were typically tightly ensconced in coral, making them virtually impossible to dislodge—they weren't going anywhere.

Only Felix and I were interested in adding these beautiful giant specimens to our shell collections, but Royce, the best diver of the three of us, volunteered to help us bring them to shore if I could only figure out how to get them up. We agreed to retrieve one of the clams the next day if possible, which gave me very little time to devise a strategy.

We returned the following day during lunchtime, and I was ready. I had located an abandoned 42-gallon fuel drum with a small, one-inch hole in what was to be the bottom end of my improvised hoisting device. I wrapped a long piece of heavy rope several times around the bottom of the barrel and formed two six-inch rope loops projecting downward. Once the barrel was in position, I planned to secure the clam to these loops.

**Giant Killer Clam found in Kwajalein lagoon**

We motored out in our small boat and anchored over the clams. I then filled the drum with water until it sank. Now all I had to do was to convince the clam to close, lash it to the barrel, pump air into the barrel, and voilà, it would pop to the surface.

The legends responsible for its nickname, killer clam, just did not fit my intended scenario. Having watched too many adventure movies as a kid, I envisioned that these monsters stalked unsuspecting divers of the deep and, without warning, pounced and clamped down on their victims, subjecting them to a horrible and painful end. Now, as I tried to encourage the fellow before me to close, my unanticipated concern was that I would run through my sixty-minute air supply before I could achieve even this first step of my plan. Each time I tickled the clam with a gloved hand it would reluctantly respond by closing an additional half inch. Fifteen minutes later it finally closed far enough that I was able to run my rope beneath it and through my prepared loops attached to the barrel. By the time I had secured the clam, half my dive time had elapsed.

My rough calculations were as follows: the weight of the clam was probably around 250 pounds, but with a density somewhere around 2.3, it would weigh on the order of 140 pounds underwater. This meant I had to arrange for at least 140 pounds of lift to accomplish my objective. Since seawater weighs 8.5 pounds per gallon, I would need to displace 16 gallons of seawater with air in my 42-gallon barrel to achieve the minimum 140 pounds of lift (enough air to displace 40 percent of the barrel's capacity).

I had brought along a spare scuba air tank for just this purpose, so I proceeded to release air from the tank in through the hole at the bottom of the barrel.

"Yes!" I thought, "Finally the clam is beginning to budge." Slowly "we" (I was hanging on to the barrel/clam combination) began to ascend. Just then I realized that my gloved hand had inadvertently become entangled in the rope securing the barrel. "No problem," I thought, "I'll ride it out and take care of that little annoyance when we reach the surface."

Oops. Another little law of physics I had overlooked. In sixty feet of water, the pressure is three atmospheres (forty-five pounds per square inch). This little detail meant that as we traveled upward into shallower water, the air in the barrel expanded to eventually occupy the entire 42 gallon volume of the barrel. Thus, 140 pounds of lifting power at the bottom would increase to nearly 400 pounds of lifting power as we neared the surface, so the barrel/shell/diver-combination speed dramatically increased as we rose.

Fortunately drag in water increases very rapidly with velocity, so we did not reach escape velocity. It was fast enough, though, to rip my mask from my face just before we broke the surface. I did manage to keep my composure and exhaled continuously as we rose to prevent my lungs from rupturing (air embolism). Once I reached the surface, the rope ensnaring my gloved hand slackened, freeing my hand.

The rest was a piece of cake. We towed my prize to shore and dragged it onto a deserted beach. Royce lashed his diving knife to the end of a broom handle and wedged it in between the imperfect meeting of the clam's two opposing halves. When mature, this is one of the few bi-valves unable to close completely, so significant gaps are always present. With his diving knife and knowledge of clam anatomy, Royce was able to cut the adductor muscle, which held the halves together.

Upon opening the shell, Royce harvested the six-pound adductor muscle as a gift for some Marshallese friends who highly prized this delicacy. The remaining guts were discarded, as they had no use. Then we placed the shell in the sun to begin its three-day curing period. There was a great deal of growth on the exterior of the shell, whose eventual strong odor from its decay could only be mitigated by long exposures in the sun and hourly doses of full-strength Clorox. (I used three gallons in the process.)

The shell is now prominently displayed in my living room. Had I realized how endangered these shells were destined to become when I harvested it in 1965, I would have left it undisturbed. The reason this did not cross my mind at the time was that a month earlier, I had observed a hundred such shells (albeit most smaller than mine) on the pier crated and ready for export—at that time they were considered abundant and certainly not endangered. My understanding is that these shells are now protected and, as such, can no longer be exported to the United States without special permits.

Twenty-five years later.

"Daddy," (daughter #5, first grade, speaking), "we're supposed to bring a seashell to class tomorrow and all I can find is this little one." She held up a one-inch snakehead cowry. "Brian brought in a *great* big one," she said exasperatedly, indicating a shell about the size of her fist.

"OK, sweetie. Let me see what I can find—see me in the morning."

The next morning, when she saw the thirty-six-inch killer-clam shell on her wagon ready to be loaded into our van (and then to her class), her eyes became nearly as large as the clamshell. The young lady was most pleased.

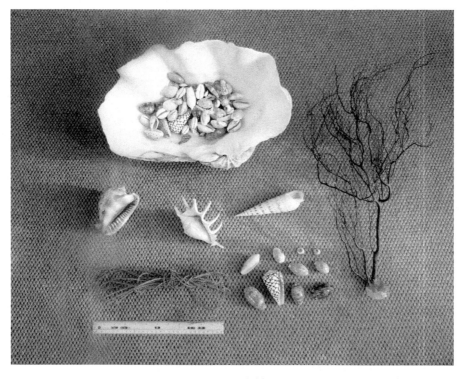

**Diving souvenirs--shells and black coral**

# 12

# GEOLOGY/GEOGRAPHY

## Atoll Formation 101

Although short on details, Darwin's theory on how atolls were formed by coral growth aided by wind and rain erosion was a good start. Imagine how well he could have extended his theory had he known about the changing sea levels due to the earth's plate tectonics and glacier growth cycles!

A growing volcanic mountain pokes above sea level to form a new high island.

Wind and rain wear down the peak, softening its overall profile.

Coral thrives in the top sixty feet of sun-exposed water hugging the coast of this new island. During eras of rising sea level due to melting glaciers and polar ice, coral, reaching for the sun, grows atop deeper skeletal coral, keeping pace with the rising sea. The mountaintop highlands continue to erode from wind and rain.

In other eras, the sea level drops as glaciers and polar caps expand, exposing the topmost layers of coral to the hostile air and direct sunlight; they die in the process. Over the millennia, erosion and wave action reduce this dead coral to sand. The coral continues to grow in the top sixty feet of water, but most progress during this phase is outward, away from the center of the island. During periods of glaciers retreat, the remaining coral extends upward once again. Through numerous repetitions of this cycle, the sandy areas gradually expand and acquire vegetation, the live coral grows outward, and the central mountain wears away, leaving a lagoon at most a few hundred feet deep.

Marine activity also plays a role in the formation of atolls. For example, parrotfish bite off small chunks of live coral, which they process for nutrients, and then they excrete sand.

The first stage, where a central mountain is hugged by new growth coral, is referred to as a high island. The middle stage, where the mountain is partially eroded and the growing/dying coral reef progressively migrates farther offshore, leaving a water-covered gap between the central mass and outer reefs, is referred to as a barrier reef. The final stage, where the central mountain erodes completely down while reef-building coral continues to grow, sustaining low, mostly vegetated islands encircling a shallow lagoon, becomes a full-fledged atoll.

There are numerous examples where a still-active atoll is totally submerged by a few feet of water, presenting serious navigational hazards. If the sea level were to drop ten feet or more, these oddities would once again become identifiable atolls.

Gaps between the atoll islands allow the tides to continually renew the lagoon's nutrients and flush the entire lagoon about once a week. Because of these fresh nutrients, sea life, including a high concentration of small sharks, is plentiful in and about these channels. These gaps also permit small boats to gain safe anchorage, providing inhabitants with commercial communication between neighboring atolls and the outside world. Islands with no lagoons (Kili, for example) or with lagoons that lack navigable channels are at a severe handicap in this way—life there is much more difficult. Rough seas and strong trade winds often cut these lagoonless islands off from most of the outside world for months at a time.

Kwajalein is one of several atolls that lays claim to being the world's largest. "Large" is all a matter of definition. Kwajalein has the largest enclosed lagoon but not the largest area when one includes reefs beyond the island ring or atolls that, as mentioned above, are totally submerged.

Coral heads, which are isolated vertical coral growths five to fifty feet across, are scattered throughout most lagoons and pose serious navigational hazards—but do provide good diving opportunities. When a Marshallese ship sails in a lagoon, the captain stations one or two seamen high in the rigging to scout for coral heads and relay their sightings to the helmsman.

Travel between atolls in the 1960s and 1970s was difficult for most Marshallese once the navy pulled out and even more difficult for the Kwajalein residents due to the lack of ships and able Marshallese captains. Early on I was told by those in the know, "If you ever have a chance to visit the outer islands on a Marshallese ship, only go with Captain Felix DeBrum on his ketch, the *Louisa.*" During my tours on Kwaj, he was the only Marshallese skipper to have never lost a ship. In fact, some captains seemed to make it a regular habit of running their boats up onto a reef every few years. Sticking with Captain Felix DeBrum proved to be prudent advice, as I discovered firsthand on my own ten-day trip to several of the outer Marshall Islands with him on the *Louisa.* (In the Marshall Islands, DeBrum is often spelled deBrum.)

# 13

# Dogs

## Kwaj Breed

Prior to my 1964 arrival on Kwaj, a few dogs and cats had been brought onto the island as pets. By the time I moved there, a ban had been introduced restricting further importation of both dogs and cats. Although no one denied that pets had personal value, the administration felt that the nuisance of having dogs at the test site outweighed the benefit of their presence. Several years following my departure, the outright ban was replaced with a cap of 110 dogs and 240 cats.

With very little new blood, the existing dog population evolved into what can only be called the "Kwaj breed." One old dog, McGoo, epitomized this breed. He looked like a typical overweight, round-ish midwestern mutt with legs borrowed from an undernourished dachshund. We used to say, "His legs are so short they barely reach the ground." Every newcomer to Kwaj, encountering McGoo for the first time, would invariably exclaim, "What kind of dog is that?" or sometimes, "Is that actually a real dog?"

In 1964 there were half a dozen younger McGoos scattered around the island. A policy of neutering all Kwaj dogs eventually led to the demise of what I'm sure would have been recognized by the American Kennel Club as its breed number 156.

## Roi Loyalty

On the work island of Roi to the north, the half-dozen resident dogs were of the garden variety. They mostly attached themselves to individual bachelors living on the island. Since a bachelor's tour would last on average about three years, a transfer adoption would inevitably take place upon an owner's departure. Some transitions were smooth, while others clearly were heart wrenching for the dog and all who witnessed the dog's suffering.

Dave had a motor scooter and a nondescript dog named Randy—both of which he had to leave behind when he completed his final tour. Dave would never putter around the island without Randy at his station, perched between his legs on the motor scooter. After Dave left, Randy resisted transferring his loyalty to anyone new and would spend entire days lying next to and guarding the defunct motor scooter.

Since the motor scooter was no longer operative, Dave's friends decided to hide it behind a storage shed in order to encourage Randy to find his next "best friend." No one saw Randy for the next few days, until someone discovered him behind the shed, once again guarding the abandoned motor scooter.

They moved the scooter again and threw it into the dump at the far end of the island. Again Randy disappeared, and again they found him faithfully guarding it at the dump. Finally they took drastic action. They took the scooter to the welding shop, cut it into thirty pieces, and scattered the pieces evenly throughout the island and in the lagoon. Two days later, a very skinny and weak Randy made his selection and adopted his new lifelong companion.

**Dog loyalty on Roi**

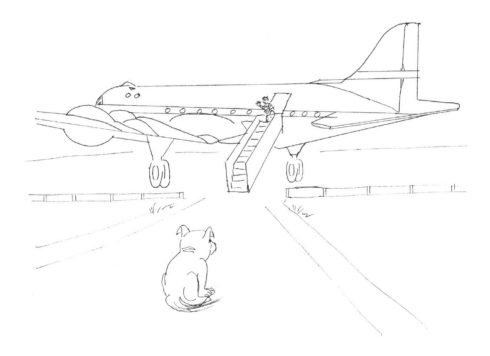

**Dog forgiveness on Roi**

## FORGIVENESS

Mickey lived on Kwajalein and, like many of his associates, commuted six days a week to Roi. As head of technical maintenance on Roi, he was issued a three-wheeled Cushman motor scooter to make his rounds.

Rascal, Mickey's constant Roi companion, waited for him at the bottom of the exit stairs precisely at 7:41 a.m. six mornings a week with tail in maximum wag mode. Rascal knew not to expect Sunday visits, making it Rascal's day of rest as well as Mickey's. Each of the other six days, Mickey would exit the plane, bound down the ramp to give Rascal a hug, trade obligatory face-licks, and then the two of them would jump onto the three-wheeler for the day's activities.

After three years with no vacation, Mickey finally decided that to save a marriage, he'd better take a month-long leave with his wife. Every day except Sunday, Rascal would meet the plane at the prescribed time but, finding no Mickey, would slink off with tail dragging and head bent low.

Finally—the big day—Mickey returned. There was Rascal waiting at the bottom of the ramp as usual. Mickey ran down the ramp and rushed over to Rascal with arms stretched out in anticipation of the big reunion hug. Rascal walked up to Mickey, looked him straight in the eye, turned, and walked away with head held proud.

It was three days before Rascal forgave Mickey.

## ROI FISHING DOGS

The famous Roi fishing dogs were not just ordinary fish-fishing dogs but hardcore shark-fishing, or perhaps more appropriately, shark-hunting dogs. Tom and Jerry, two midsized Roi mutts, developed their team-shark-fishing skills on their own. The wolf packs of the wild north hunting their prey had nothing on these two.

During the bimonthly extra-low tides, several hundred feet of shoreline reefs would be exposed for a few hours twice a day—except for the numerous shallow sand-bottomed channels extending from the shore out to where the reef dropped off into deeper water. The sun was a formidable deterrent in preventing larger coral life forms from taking hold in this exposed transitional zone. Some very small plant life, however, had adapted to survive through the few hours of low tide, so the exposed portion of the reef was not entirely devoid of life.

The small fish that inhabited this portion of the reef were restricted to the channels and small pools that retained water during these periods of extra-low ebb tides until the ocean returned to its normal level.

This low-tide concentration of small fish in the restricted channels enabled small sharks to profitably hunt the then-defenseless prey. In fact, on more than one occasion while wading the reef at low tide, I had a small, two-foot shark dart between my legs in pursuit of his lunch. This can be a rather unnerving experience the first time it happens; however, after a few months, an experienced reef wader would think, "Ho hum, another shark between my legs."

As the sharks hunted the small fish, Tom and Jerry hunted the sharks. One of the pair played sentinel near the shore end of a proven channel, where it shallowed to only a few inches, while his spotting partner would station himself near the deeper end of the channel. Once the spotter identified a potential victim, he would jump in behind the shark and make as much commotion as he could. On most hunts, the shark immediately attempted to escape the turmoil by sprinting up the channel toward shore. The chase dog would then pursue the shark, driving him into the more and more restricted shallow portion of the channel. Meanwhile, the partner dog, waiting patiently right at the spot where the shark virtually ran out of room, would pounce and, in a single swoop, drag the shark out of the water onto the exposed reef.

Hunt successfully concluded—well, at least most of the time. Since Tom was missing two toes off his right paw, it seems he may have misjudged his victim on at least one occasion—perhaps during the early phase of their self-taught shark-hunting trials.

**Denizens of the deep are no match
for denizens of the shallows**

# 14

# OTHER PETS

## DAUGHTER SEE, DAUGHTER DO

The boldest pet caper on Kwaj I remember was when Scott smuggled a monkey onto Kwajalein. I couldn't believe his gall, keeping Billy, his newly acquired baby monkey, in a cardboard box under his seat during the eleven-hour MATS (Military Air Transport Service) flight from Hickam Air Force Base in Honolulu to Kwajalein.

Billy and their baby daughter, Tina, became great playmates, entertaining themselves for hours scampering around their trailer together. Scott and Mary were amused at most of their joint antics until they realized Tina was beginning to copy their monkey's activities a little too closely. It was when their daughter tried to chase and eat cockroaches that they decided the two of them needed closer monitoring.

Sadly, Billy got into some pest control poison and died a few months after their arrival—fortunately, that was a fate from which Tina was spared.

## TURTLE

Kwajalein is surrounded by water and occupied by adventurers, so it was inevitable that eventually various indigenous seawater creatures would become pets, at least on a trial basis. During a day of snorkeling, Alex spotted and captured a small, four-inch green sea turtle. He kept it in his trailer and fed it well. One evening after it had grown to sixteen inches, he decided his pet needed more water time, so he took it to the saltwater Dependents' Pool. As it was after seven, the pool was nearly empty of swimmers, and the lifeguard had left for the day. After five minutes of uneventful "turtle playtime," an older woman at the pool spotted the turtle.

Alex was perplexed by her scream and irrational fear of swimming with a friendly pet turtle. No amount of explanation or consoling had any effect. To this traumatized woman, it was as if the owner of a great white shark were explaining to her, "Oh, don't worry, he seldom eats swimmers." Or as an owner of a boa constrictor might rationalize, "It's not a problem. She's already eaten a rat and two kittens today." Needless to say, that was Alex's one and only foray to the pool with his pet.

## WALKING ONE'S PET

Mel tried to walk his pet down the hall. Granted, his pet had a leash so it couldn't stray too far, but it didn't seem to take well to his master's intentions. After two days Mel gave up and released his pet back into the wild. "Ya know," he told his friends later, "these eight-inch coconut crabs really don't make good pets."

My oldest daughter, two and a half at the time, reached a similar conclusion after she failed in her attempt to make seventy-five small hermit crabs her pets at a seldom-visited beach. The full extent of their pet tricks was to use their claws to seal up their protective doors or alternatively just wander off. Hermit crab races proved futile, and their tickling of a child's open palm when attempting to scamper off had limited amusement value. My daughter did refer to them as tickle bugs because of their palm-tickling effects.

Unbeknownst to her at the time, hermit crabs are not cute little creatures but ferocious killers. Given a chance, they will attack and rip apart another hermit crab to gain access to and occupy the adversary's shell-house.

## FISH TANKS

There were two water systems on Kwaj, which fed every housing unit—freshwater for most domestic needs and saltwater for the toilets. This dual water system made complete sense, as freshwater was in limited supply and saltwater was unlimited.

The distribution of saltwater to each home enabled residents to keep large aquariums, up to one-hundred-gallon capacity, stocked with local exotic and relatively rare tropical fish. If any of these owners had valued their saltwater fish at stateside retail prices, their collections would easily have been worth several thousand dollars.

Jim and Sara went beyond just collecting fish; they also had several eels in their tank. Sara rose one night to use the bathroom in her bare feet but in her groggy half-asleep state, missed the turn and wandered past her aquarium. It was then that she remembered the rule, "Always keep a lid on any fish tank harboring live eels."

*Squish!*

## Cats

The single biggest problem with having a cat on Kwajalein was that the owners would often become so attached that they couldn't think of abandoning the littlest family member when eventually returning stateside. The choice was take the cat home and pay the fees (transportation expenses, shots, and long quarantine costs) or use the money to send their child to college.

# 15

# WHERE ARE THE SOCIOLOGISTS?

Place several hundred relatively young, well-educated, and very highly paid scientists and their families on an island supported by another three thousand bachelors; take away all private cars, TVs, and off-island phone service; give them all too much money with nothing to spend it on; and you're left with enough material for at least fifty PhD sociologist and psychologist theses.

For example, the commanding colonel's wife, representing the pinnacle of the island's society, felt it her duty to upgrade the island's moral standards. To this end, she persuaded her husband to ban *Playboy*. The ensuing bachelor rebellion squashed her good intentions in about fifteen minutes. If she couldn't keep *Playboy* out of her son's hands, there was no way she could single-handedly keep it away from three thousand very lonely, lovelorn bachelors.

Too often, research projects suffer from too many highly correlated variables whose cross effects have to be backed out to analyze a variable of interest. On Kwajalein, many of these extraneous variables were missing to begin with. The remaining variables became more prominent under these circumstances and thus, much easier to study.

Women with seemingly "average status" stateside often seized the opportunity to elbow their way into the top echelons of Kwaj society, albeit for a fleeting, tour-limited half-life. On the other hand, stateside "high-status" women often passed up the opportunity of being a big fish in a little pond and preferred to withdraw from social prominence. Instead, they devoted time to self-improvement or efforts to assist Marshallese with education, religious issues, or health needs rather than worry about frivolous social endeavors.

While not actually specified as mandatory, our site manager strongly implied what was expected from us by his statement—"There will be a reception for Colonel Blah-blah-blah tomorrow night, and of course I expect all of you to attend." I've never done well with veiled threats based on other people's social obligations, so I went to a movie instead. When the lights came on, we found two other couples from our company who had responded in the same manner. Engineers tend to have maverick streaks—or as I'd prefer to construe it—engineers are independent thinkers.

The most hurtful type of nouveau socialite is the one who enthusiastically boasts to a neighbor about a great party she is planning and about which important people will be attending, and then does not invite the neighbor. This happened to us on more than one occasion.

## MONDAY

"Can I borrow some of your patio chairs? We're having a few friends over for a small get-together Saturday night."

## WEDNESDAY

"Jimmy (the best bachelor-cook on the island) said he would cook for our party. Aren't we lucky?"

## EARLY THURSDAY

"Al promised he would bring his group to play for us. I just wanted to let you know the music might be a bit loud. If it gets too out of hand, let us know and we'll try to tone it down a bit."

## LATE THURSDAY

"At least thirty-five people have accepted their invitations including both the Lieutenant Colonel Brigs (second in command on the island) and Frank (the site manager)—it's going to be a great party!"

## Friday

More of the same but no invitation.

## Saturday

Party occurs.

## Sunday

Recaps success of party but shows no remorse at not having invited the neighbor. Implication: "You're not important enough for me, but I still find you useful to discuss my success."

In J.M. Barrie's book, *The Admirable Crichton*, an elite family is shipwrecked along with a few of their servants on a remote deserted island. After a few weeks it became clear that rescue was problematic and the little group had better concentrate on their independent survival. As a result, the social order flipped. The butler, with the largest practical skill set of the entire group, assumed control and quickly defined the top of the social order.

Life changes on Kwajalein were not as drastic as being shipwrecked, but many aspects of social order were altered, owing to the new metrics of opportunity, perceived importance, and ability. Social climbers had to adjust to old realities once they returned home.

# 16

# HOUSING—SORTA

Housing allocations were based on a vague combination of military rank or equivalent GS rating, need, and perceived importance. The higher ranks were allowed to bring their families and lived in two- or three-bedroom cinderblock duplexes or in three-bedroom fifty-by-ten-foot trailers in an area nicknamed "Silver City" due to the shiny aluminum exteriors. The more highly ranked (GS-11 and above) personnel on bachelor status resided in BQs (bachelors' quarters) and were assigned one, two, or four to a room depending on rank, while the lesser-ranked bachelors resided in denser, more Spartan housing that reminded me of a school dorm.

Large families with up to five children found it challenging to squeeze into a two-bedroom duplex (the few three-bedroom houses were reserved for families with six or more children), but with a great deal of creativity somehow managed to pull it off. One family with five daughters discarded all of their bedroom furniture except for two sets of drawers. They covered the remaining floor area with wall-to-wall mattresses. The only turf wars that erupted were over the time and space allocation of the most valued real estate in the house, the single bathroom. With six women in the house, I suspect the father often found it prudent to utilize the great outdoors as his emergency backup.

**55x10 Trailer In Silver City**

**Typical two bedroom duplex**

When the decision was made to change Kwajalein's primary mission to supporting missile-reentry research, it became necessary to ramp up the size and scope of the facilities. At that time, most of the housing allotment was based on remnants of military protocol, with the concept of separate but equal housing and dining (some equals being more equal than other equals).

The military soon discovered a defect in their housing allocation algorithm, as their criteria for determining "equivalent military rank" was heavily dependent on income. The pay of the lowest workers, highly inflated due to their 25 percent hardship-premium pay and extra hours of guaranteed overtime, put many of them in a pay grade as high as a captain (and the captain had to pay federal income tax while the ditch digger did not). This pay equivalency presented a conundrum in that coveted housing could be usurped by highly paid ditch diggers—not in the military's best interest.

In the end, the whole issue was sidestepped by giving each corporation represented on the island their own housing allotment and letting them handle the more complex assignment details. Problem? What problem?

Couples who considered themselves an "item" but were not officially married, tied the "knot of convenience" just so they could both work and qualify for decent housing. Other than dependents and a few teachers, there were no single female personnel on Kwaj at that time (our typist from the Kelly Girl temp agency was a young, 260-pound Hawaiian male). Some convenience-couples probably reversed their marital state at the end of their tours.

Each company with employees on Kwajalein had their own compensation packages. Housing expenses were usually covered by a per diem allowance. A bachelor's per diem also included the mess-hall food, which, if not gourmet, was better than I expected and was certainly better than dorm food. Snack-bar expenses were not covered.

# 17

# SHIPS, SHELLS, AND SHARKS

I was deeply engrossed examining the Noritake china before me—a couple of plates and a Noritake ashtray (I had no idea Noritake included ashtrays in their china sets) and as such, did not notice Pete approaching me from behind until he tapped me on the shoulder. I turned to face him and...

I am sure at this point the reader has formed an image of me shopping in the china section of a high-end department store when a friend solicits my attention, perhaps to inquire if I'd wish to join him for a latte.

Best I continue.

There was Pete, holding a human femur in his outstretched hand, which he had just used to get my attention. After a bit of a start, I acknowledged his discovery, at which point he swam back and returned it to its rightful owner to make him, or at least his skeleton, whole once more. Seasoned divers are very respectful of human remains and wish to leave them undisturbed. In this case, however, I suspect Pete wanted to ensure a lamenting ghost would not manifest itself in front of his trailer at midnight wailing, "Where's my missing leg? Where's my missing leaaag? I want my leaaaaaag back." (Note—ghosts tend not to be very sophisticated in their wailing and never seem to lament the loss of their femur.)

Shock over, I returned to sifting through the scattered debris in the galley of the sunken ship in an attempt to locate additional Noritake dishes or any other interesting artifacts (excluding bones of course). Pete's find was the only human remains we came across in all our many dives on this ship.

The ship, perhaps two hundred feet in length, rested upright in 120 feet of water. What was left of its control bridge was less than twenty feet below the surface and could be observed from the air if one knew where to look. The best way to spot it was from the window of our C-47 (the civilian version was called the DC-3) commuter plane during its final approach to the Roi-Namur runway.

Most "Kwajalein-to-Roi-Namur" commuters have no idea what they are looking at when they scan the lagoon during their first few flights. They are still newbies. After their twentieth flight, their mindset morphs to that of an old timer and they usually stop looking out the window altogether.

The four of us—Royce, Pete, Felix, and I—decided that we had to check out this light blue spot in the lagoon to verify for ourselves whether or not the rumor that it marked the location of a sunken medium-sized cargo ship was true.

We never actually entered the water during our first lunchtime excursion, as it took us the entire time just to locate the ship in our Boston whaler and fix its bearings relative to the neighboring islands. Once that had been accomplished, locating it on subsequent trips was a piece of cake.

On future forays, it took less than half an hour for us to dash from our offices, load our equipment, motor to the ship, moor to its control bridge, and begin our dive. This gave us forty minutes, or just less than one tank of air, to dive on, above, and into the sunken ship before heading back to work. Most of our interest was focused on depths between forty and sixty feet, so during our weekly lunch/diving "hour," we were able to explore without concern about entering into the decompression diving tables—which occur when diving too long and too deep (sixty minutes at sixty feet is an example of one such limit).

There were some signs that other divers had been on the scene and previously salvaged a few of the more accessible artifacts, but mostly, it was virgin territory. Exercising caution, we never probed beyond two cabins into the depths of the vessel. Divers who wish to penetrate deeper than twenty feet into a sunken hull must plan their forays very carefully and rely on trailing lines strung behind them as they enter to ensure they can retrace their route when they wish to exit.

A few months after we began our lunchtime ship exploration dives near Roi, two divers perished while diving on the capsized 681-foot *Prinz Eugen*, a World War II German heavy-cruiser war prize (accompanying ship to the *Bismarck*). Following its participation in two nuclear assessment tests at Bikini Atoll, the *Prinz Eugen* was towed to the Kwajalein lagoon, where it inadvertently sank during a December storm in 1946. Its resting place in relatively shallow water just off Ennubuj (also referred to as Carlson), two miles north of Kwaj proper, made it an ideal local diving destination. The two divers who lost their lives had wandered too deep into the inner maze of cabins and passageways without using trailing safety lines, became disoriented (the ship was upside down) and ultimately ran out of air before any of their accompanying divers could rescue them.

I spent most of my weekly dives sifting through the debris in the galley, one room in—far enough in for me. An open door and two hatches provided plenty of light and accessibility, especially as the water was relatively clear with good visibility when I first entered. Twelve to sixteen inches of debris blanketed the floor—detritus from twenty-five years of decaying wood and furnishings. Shortly after I entered the galley, my flippers would stir up the debris to the point where visibility was reduced to a few inches. As long as there continued to be sufficient light, I proceeded with my search while attempting to maintain my orientation—always a challenge.

After fifteen minutes moiling about the room, the debris suspension became so thick that the directionality of light scattering from the doors faded and obscured even my exit direction. To find my way out, I rose to the room's ceiling, where the top three inches were less disturbed than the rest of the room. This enabled me to get a fix on the direction from which the door light emanated and thus identify my escape route.

Positioning myself at the top of the galley had to be done with considerable care. Loose cables and hanging debris in this region threatened to entangle the hose of my scuba gear. I moved very slowly and very deliberately when attempting this maneuver. It was the only real danger of my entire dive.

We made at least twenty dives on the ship throughout the next year, during which I recovered several Noritake dishes, an ashtray, a hand-blown bottle containing a clamshell three times the width of the bottle's neck (it had grown inside the bottle), two sixty-pound brass portholes, two large navigation lanterns and a three-inch cartridge shell. Actually, Felix salvaged the shell along with two others from a munitions storage locker he pried open near the ship's single defensive gun at the bow. He pulled out the cordite to disarm it while underwater—not such a smart thing to do, as this explosive material becomes very unstable after a few decades, even when submerged. We left a few portholes for future divers and the internal cabins were never touched—that is, not by us. After a while, our dives became routine and even though we occasionally brought a guest or two, including our site manager, the four of us remained the local ship-diving experts.

Another oddity of this ship's location was the sharks—or rather the lack thereof. During my five years diving in the lagoon, I was accompanied one time or another by hundreds of sharks––everywhere, that is, except in the vicinity of this ship. Yet, during this same interval, the only time I ever encountered barracudas was during my ship dives.

This originally English ship had been moored in Singapore (best guess) on December 8, 1941, when the Japanese attacked the British fleet simultaneously with their attack on Pearl Harbor. The Japanese captured it when Singapore fell a few weeks later (my future father-in-law, Enlin Pan, was staying at the Singapore Raffles Hotel on the very day of the attack and escaped on the last plane to leave the city twenty-three days later). We discovered that many of the brass labels had English inscriptions on their reverse sides. Following the ship's capture, the Japanese merely reversed the labels and reinscribed them in their own language.

Confirming her propensity for being in the wrong place at the wrong time, this ship was moored in the Kwajalein Lagoon a mile offshore from Roi-Namur when the American battleships began their February 1944 bunker-softening-up barrage. This time she did not survive.

Souvenir gathering on such ships is restricted today, but this was a period of exploration before anyone gave such conservation ideas any thought.

I suspect the control bridge to which we secured our dive boat has long been reclaimed by the corrosive action of the ocean, and after forty-five years, it is probable that other divers have mapped all the details of the ship. Hopefully, what is left is still providing enjoyment to present-day explorers.

**Portholes, shell casing and
lantern from sunken ship**

**Shell in a bottle found in galley of sunken ship**

# 18

# THE HERO

## ROYCE AND PETE AGAIN

"Whatever your motivation," exclaimed Royce, "I consider you a hero and credit you with saving my life—or at least my leg."

"Pete, that makes you a hero," chimed in two friends.

"No way—a hero does something 'cause he's brave. What I did seemed more like stupidity to me. I didn't think, I just did—just a reaction. If I had thought about it for even two seconds, I would have played it safe and stayed in the boat."

More friends gathered around to listen to the play-by-play account of the shark encounter. They all agreed—Pete was a hero.

Pete and Royce had gone on a short dive about a half mile off Roi's shore during their lunch break. They did not go looking for anything in particular but simply wanted to enjoy a quick and relaxed dive. They found themselves lolling around among the little, colorful tropical reef fish that populated a small coral head. These fish are experts on their immediate neighborhood but panic if they are forced even six feet away from their home in any direction. If you try to herd them away, they swim furiously to return to their familiar home, as if they would rather die at home than forge into unfamiliar waters. In their first half hour of diving, Pete and Royce strayed no further than fifty yards from their anchored boat—considered a normal, safe exploration range.

A relatively small, five-foot blacktip shark swam by a couple of times—not that unusual—and was of no immediate concern. However, on its third pass, the shark demonstrated an aggressive behavior that caught both Pete and Royce's attention. That was when Pete noticed blood coming from Royce's shoulder—he had probably unknowingly scraped it on a piece of coral. They poked their heads out of the water long enough for Pete to tell Royce, "Royce, you're bleeding and I don't like this guy's attitude. Best head back to the boat and call it a day."

Royce nodded, and they both began to swim back toward the boat. Pete reached the boat first, clambered over the gunwale, and shed his tank. During his return swim, the shark had made closer and closer passes, even bumping Pete at one point to test the worthiness of its potential target.

"Just as Royce was reaching for the boat, I saw the shark alter his tactics and head straight for him. I knew instinctively that this pass was not a practice run but the real thing.

"I couldn't control myself. It was an impulse. In retrospect, it seems completely insane. I leaped out of the boat with both feet landing squarely on top of the shark when he was hardly three feet away from Royce. He was completely startled and took off like a shot. We both managed to scramble back into the boat just before he returned."

The frenzied shark was not to be denied after he had invested so much time and effort laying all that groundwork to secure dinner. He (maybe she) rammed the boat several times as he thrashed about in a last-ditch effort to gain his objective. This was one angry shark, but luckily, one that was too small to capsize or even to damage the boat.

# 19

# A FEW SHARK ENCOUNTERS

## First Dive on Kwaj, First Kwaj Shark, and First "With Friends Like These, Who Needs Enemies?"

We had been diving for thirty minutes—my very first Kwajalein dive. My snorkeling buddy, Tom, was checking me out to ensure I had sufficient aquatic abilities to qualify for the on-island NAUI diving course. Everything was fine until he spotted a six-foot nurse shark cruising our way. Although Tom knew it was not menacing, he did not want me to become startled if I spotted it on my own, so he decided to alert me to its presence.

I was ascending from a shallow twenty-five-foot dive as he reached down his flipper to tap me on my shoulder. Then the following happened in rapid succession:

I looked up and spotted the shark.

Tom's outstretched leg missed my shoulder.

Tom's outstretched leg partially knocked my mask off.

My mask filled with water, basically rendering me blind.

I was left confused with no vision and had an image etched into both of my retinas of a two-hundred-foot shark racing straight toward me.

So "with friends like these…"

Oops, Mother Nature to the Rescue

I was not doing a particularly deep free dive, only 50 feet. To put this in perspective, I had a few friends who could free dive to 120 feet and do useful work down to 60 feet, whereas my deepest free dive was barely 80 feet. I figured I could linger on the bottom for twenty seconds of this 50-foot dive and still have a ten-to fifteen-second reserve by the time I surfaced.

I pushed off and started to swim hard toward the surface. At fifty feet, a free diver's lungs are compressed to 40 percent of maximum volume, so buoyancy on the bottom is negative by a few pounds. A diver does not regain positive buoyancy until he reaches between fifteen and twenty feet.

All was going as planned, when a game changer appeared in the form of a couple five-foot sharks who exhibited more interest in me than I was comfortable with.

Dilemma—to discourage a shark from categorizing you as a potential food source, it is best if you swim slowly toward her (or him) to demonstrate total lack of fear. As you approach, you mind-meld with the shark and communicate, "Look at me, Ms. Shark. Notice I am just as big as you are with one very scary oversized eye—clearly I am an efficient predator. I also have two long tentacles that would inflict serious damage should you attack. In fact, should you hang around too long, I may decide you are worth eating. Best you leave—and warn your buddies about me."

Problem—with twenty seconds of reserve air in my lungs, this maneuver of leveling off and showing the sharks who was boss can only be executed at most two times.

Solution—Mother Nature to the rescue. With adrenalin pumping to the max, I suddenly became convinced that I had hours of reserve. No problem. After four leveling maneuvers, everything worked out just fine.

## Cowboy Dave

"So just how difficult could it be?" thought Dave, "you just slip a lasso around a sleeping nurse shark's tail, and when he takes off, you hang on tight and get a thrilling ride. It isn't as if I'm trying to water ski like in the cartoons—I'm just going for a short ride. It'll be a hoot."

Dave knew just where he could find a sleeping shark. He had his rope ready, and made sure to wear gloves to protect his hands against possible friction burns. He didn't want any possibility of bleeding. Bleeding? Not good.

Cowboy Dave located his unsuspecting ride—a six-foot nurse shark asleep in a cave—and very carefully placed the rope's slip-knot over its tail. He was about to yank on it to wake the shark when the shark rewrote the scenario. The tail had not moved an inch, but the shark's head had turned to the point where it was staring Dave straight in the eye less than a foot away. Dave had no idea that sharks were so flexible. Before Dave could even consider a plan B, whoosh, the shark was gone. Dave was confused and dis-orientated, as well as bleeding from a friction sharkskin burn on his shoulder—like sandpaper.

Dave went to plan C: "Don't play with sharks."

## Macho Man—Not

Atlen sure was impressive. He was so knowledgeable, could do almost anything, and the boat he owned back in San Diego dwarfed all the privately owned boats on Kwaj. Clearly he was a true Renaissance man—a man's man, a Macho Man.

Atlen took the diving course required of all divers who wished to scuba in the Kwajalein waters and had no trouble passing the written test, the pool test, and the lagoon checkout dive, which took place in a sheltered, benign locale.

During the qualifying dive required for his scuba certification, Atlen was quite generous in sharing with his associates stories about his previous diving exploits in exotic places around the world, including dangerous situations and encounters with denizens of the deep.

For his first dive after earning his diving certificate, he chose to join a group of divers bound for the Meck Channel (off the northern end of Meck Island). With a show of great confidence and bravado, he flipped into the water with his diving buddy to begin the adventure. Fifteen seconds later Atlen was back in the boat.

"Sharks! Sharks everywhere! Oh my god, so many sharks."

No one had prepared him for this. One or two small sharks maybe, but not dozens of medium-sized (huge to him) sharks. Meck Channel was known to have the highest density of shark activity in the entire Kwajalein atoll, as that was where the most shark food sources were to be found.

Once in the water, Atlen was startled to discover such a high level of shark activity surrounding him. He climbed back into the boat as quickly as he could and remained there until they returned to shore two hours later. He never dove, snorkeled, or even waded again during the remainder of his tour.

Remove "Macho Man" from his list of descriptors.

(See chapter 30 for more adventures of "Macho Man—Not.")

# 20

# BENEVOLENT DICTATORSHIP

It is my belief that a benevolent dictatorship starts out as the best and most efficient form of government one could want. Unfortunately after the first week or two, its leader becomes addicted to the inherent power of a dictatorship and convinces himself he can do no wrong. Then it's all downhill from there.

On Kwajalein, first the navy and then the army was in charge of the overall administration of the island, island contractors, and related logistics. Since nearly all of the major decisions were handled in Washington, only a small contingent of the military and their dependents were actually needed on Kwaj—perhaps thirty in all, much less than even 1 percent of the entire population.

The army held weekly meetings with the site managers and major contractor representatives in order to update them on the latest island happenings, discuss common issues, and solicit input and feedback.

Returning from one such meeting, our site manager explained, "Lynn, this may surprise you, but the army really does have our best interests at heart."

"Larry, I have no doubt that that is their intention, but that is not where the problem lies. The problem is that they are basing their decision-making processes about our 'best interests' with very little input from us and with a heavy dose of army culture. From their position, it is natural for them to make sure that above all else, they look good to their superiors and to the public in general. Remember, they control the newspaper and the radio station on this island. It is a matter of looking good and collecting 'atta-boys' so they can move on and up. Plus, the military is accustomed to running installations where the average education level is slightly above a high school graduate, whereas the staff members of the on-island research companies have, on average, a master's degree, if not higher. I have actually found that several of the lieutenants and captains on our little island tend to be intimidated by the Kwaj scientific community. When talking among themselves, they often refer to us as 'prima donnas.'"

Below are a few examples exposing the gap between the military culture and the culture of the scientists living and working on Kwajalein.

### EXAMPLE ONE

One day several babies became ill (not seriously) and nobody could identify the problem. A few days later it got out (it always gets out) that for a few hours, the saltwater feed was inadvertently connected to the freshwater network, which fed the dependent housing trailers. As a result, several baby bottles were made up using saltwater instead of freshwater. The army, "so as not to cause concern among the residents," suppressed this information for several days—a trait of a benevolent dictator—thereby actually causing unnecessary and prolonged worry for the residents.

### EXAMPLE TWO

A contingency of junior officers and lieutenant colonels were visiting Kwajalein for a briefing on our missile-defense research capabilities. As part of the briefing process, they joined us on our Kwaj to Roi commuter flights—but with a new wrinkle. As soon as these flights pulled up to the Roi terminal, a lieutenant would jump up and announce, "Everyone stay seated until the officers have disembarked."

This was an introduction of unfamiliar protocol to us not hitherto imposed on any of these flights. It irritated all the usual passengers who, in general, were not the type to be impressed by class status. In fact, if true rank protocol had been in effect, the average daily commuter would have outranked the average military guest aboard. On the third morning that the military implemented this protocol, the commuter passengers started to call out cadence: "Hep, two, three, four, hep, two, three, four…"

A little later that morning, one of the captains took our manager aside and asked, "Why don't they like us?"

"It's not that they don't like you. Some of these guys are world-class scientists, and your group has decided they should show respect and wait until a twenty-seven-year-old major with a bachelor's degree has asserted his supposed status-right to deplane before a PhD, retired full professor. It's just not part of our culture."

During the next two days of their visit, the officers took their turn to disembark just like everyone else and harmony prevailed.

## BROKEN FREEZER

The supply of frozen meat at "Safeway" (Kwaj's grocery store) disappeared over a two-day period. Some residents were stocking up while others, who never got the word, discovered empty meat freezers by closing time on day two. Clerks and managers at the store offered no explanations but did reassure their customers that new supplies would be arriving soon.

There was no mention of the frozen meat shortage in the *Hourglass*, our local newspaper, or during our radio's local news announcements. Two weeks later the subject was finally broached when the army praised themselves for repairing the freezers in a timely manner. They publicized the fix but not the problem, explaining their actions offline by stating they didn't want to create a possible run on the few meat products that were still in stock.

Of course what did happen was the privileged, informed few stocked up first, leaving scant leftovers for the others.

# 21

# WHERE HAS ALL THE WATER GONE?

*Hourglass* headlines halfway through the dry season:
*Water Consumption above Normal*
*Residents Asked to Conserve*

A week later, water consumption amounts were published weekly to emphasize overuse. Historic water consumption for that time of the year, 150,000 to 200,000 gallons a day, was then being exceeded by nearly 50 percent.

Two weeks later:
*Residents Not Trying Hard Enough*
*Water Fountains Replaced*
*by Coolers and Paper Cups*
*Consumption 300,000 gal/day*

By this time, the residents, at least those I knew, had concluded that there had to be a serious leak somewhere.

Runoff from Kwajalein's water catchment basin, adjacent to the 6,700-foot runway, fed a water-storage farm of fifteen water tanks, each capable of holding a million gallons. It had been mandated that three million gallons be reserved for fire protection, which left a maximum storage capacity of twelve million gallons for day-to-day industrial and domestic use. On average, three out of every four years, sufficient water was collected during the rainy season to handle the community's needs during the dry season. During the drier years, a backup diesel-driven desalinization plant provided an emergency reserve source when needed. The army was reluctant to bring this backup supply of freshwater online, as it was quite expensive and would heavily impact the island's overall budget—a policy every resident respected and supported.

We were naive at first, assuming that if a leak were suspected by the army, they would report it as such. As pleas for conservation escalated, we all did our share while waiting for the powers that be to reach the same conclusion we had and send for off-island assistance.

"How can the army keep berating us for not doing our share? I take two minute showers and reuse rinse water from doing the dishes for watering our plants."

"I agree. By now even my fourth grader is convinced there's gotta be a leak somewhere."

"My guess is it's the army's wishful thinking again. If they can blame someone else, they can hold off taking action that might make them look bad or run them over budget."

"You're right. I sometimes think the army just wished we'd all go away so they could run Kwaj their way with no interference from us."

Two weeks later:

*Domestic Water to Be Rationed*
*Limited to 3 Morning Hours and 4 Evening Hours*
*Consumption 380,000 gal/day*

(Note—toilets were not affected as they were supplied by a separate saltwater distribution network.)

The next week the army organized the elementary school children to deliver water-saving tips door to door to all residences.

"Oh thank God. I only have a PhD in physics, so I need a ten-year-old to explain to me how to save water. What is the army thinking? Why don't they just fix the damn leak and leave us out of it? Funny the *Hourglass* doesn't mention the possibility of a leak—only that we are unpatriotic citizens."

*Consumption 425,000 gal/day*
*Residents Not Doing Their Part*

Then finally and suddenly, as if the sun had set, there was no mention of a water shortage in the *Hourglass* at all. During the next three weeks there was a complete blackout—nada, nothing— the problem had never existed. This topic was no longer of interest, no longer worth reporting. Finally an article on page five acknowledged that the water shortage was no longer critical, but it was always a good idea to conserve nonetheless.

The explanation eventually filtered out. A primary underground water main had collapsed and had been spilling at least two hundred thousand gallons a day into the porous ground. To save money during the initial build of the water distribution, only a single water meter had been installed for the entire system. It was located near the water-storage farm outlet and before the break. Thus it monitored the total water usage but provided no indication as to where the water went after that.

Experts from Honolulu were finally called in and quickly solved the problem. The army had severely questioned the integrity of the residents and berated them beyond reason and as such, was too embarrassed to admit they had mismanaged the problem. It was too easy (or perhaps wishful thinking) to point an accusing finger at the users—benevolent dictatorship at work again.

Of course it was also reported in the *Hourglass* a few weeks later that the army was on top of the problem all along and was pleased with themselves for acting so decisively to rectify the situation.

# 22

# CONSEQUENCES, CONSEQUENCES, CONSEQUENCES

There are always those pesky unexpected consequences that pop up at the most inconvenient times. A particularly dramatic consequence of water rationing descended on Bob and Sally Jorgensen, who resided in one of the "Silver City" trailers.

Water delivered to the housing areas during the declared emergency shortage was turned off except during the morning rationed hours of six o'clock to nine o'clock and evening hours of four o'clock to eight o'clock. Bob and Sally understood this arrangement, but their Marshallese maid, not a big reader of our local newspaper, did not.

The Jorgensens were about to begin their month-long vacation back to the East Coast. They were packed and ready to head for the airport shortly after nine o'clock. Their maid was about to leave the trailer herself when she decided to get one last drink of water. Finding the cold-water tap did not respond, she tried the hot-water tap. Again nothing—no matter how far she turned the handle. She repeated her search for water at every water faucet in the house. Finally she gave up, but not before leaving a sponge and a few washcloths in a couple of the sinks blocking the drains. Everyone left—doors locked, trailer forgotten.

I'm sure the reader has anticipated the event I'm about to report. Several days later, a neighbor passing the Jorgensens' trailer on his way home from work saw water leaking from several doors and windows. Upon closer observation, it became obvious that an epic problem was in the making. Water was nearly four feet deep in the trailer and reached partway up the lower windows. Having no key, the neighbor alerted security, who dispatched someone to investigate twenty minutes later. The security representative explained that they did not have the authority to open the trailer, nor did they have the means to do so. The security personnel were known both as the lowest paid and the most overpaid group on the island. I suspect that if any of them had had a high school diploma, they would have been considered overqualified.

The neighbors finally convinced security to call the facilities manager and have him send someone over with the authority and the means to resolve the problem. Two hours later, after facilities and security questioned whether they should pay someone overtime to fix the problem or save money by waiting until Monday morning, or whether they even had the authority to make the decision anyway, someone did finally show up.

By now a small crowd had gathered—all eager to witness the grand opening. I did not witness the event but I can imagine the scene: scattered deck chairs ensconced with local spectators sampling martinis while munching on hors d'oeuvres waiting for the big moment.

The trailer opened. "*Whoosh!*" Contents not secured to the floor flowed with the flood into the yard. Finally the guilty water taps were turned off.

Friends and neighbors did what they could to salvage and clean the more valuable possessions, but most items stored below water level were lost.

Let's see. Ten feet by fifty-five feet by four feet by 7.5 gallons per cubic foot—that's sixteen thousand gallons—not insignificant when compared to the island's daily consumption.

**Mommy, why can't we have an indoor pool like the Browns?**

# 23

# EXTRA INCOME

## SUPPLY AND DEMAND

"Why is there a line of guys in front of that hotel room?" (The transient hotel adjacent to Kwaj airport.)

"Don't know. Maybe they're selling stuff or something."

"Strange? I thought I saw that line a couple of times last week too."

"You two guys are so dumb—the new stewardesses fly in to Kwaj twice a week, Tuesdays and Thursdays, spend the night, and fly back to Honolulu the next day."

"Oh."

The word got out. The lines got longer. Two weeks later, the army got wind of this new development and stewards replaced the stewardesses on those flights. No more lines. Problem solved, although I'm not sure there was a problem in the first place.

## BABYSITTING

Natalie hung around the bank's small lobby until it was clear of other patrons, and then tentatively approached the teller window.

"Natalie—haven't seen you for a while. Don't you usually bank by mail with our Hawaii branch? Making a deposit today, are you?"

Natalie avoided eye contact as she slid her passbook toward the teller and replied softly, "No, I'm here to close out my account."

The bank teller noticed that she seemed a bit on edge but responded with a friendly "no problem" before he even had a chance to glance at the passbook.

He picked up the passbook to check her account number, hesitated, and then excused himself with a "Pardon me, Natalie. I'll be right back."

She blurted out, "Is there a problem?"

"No, no, of course not. No problem at all. I'm assuming you would like me to cut you a cashier's check. Is that right? Oh, and do you want any of that in cash?"

"Yeah. I'd like $150 in cash please."

"Would five twenties and five tens be OK or would you like smaller bills?"

"Yeah, sure. That'll be fine."

"I'll have to cut the cashier's check on the machine in the back. Won't take but a minute."

Once in back, the teller approached his manager with, "George, Natalie Branson wants to close out her savings account."

"So what's the big deal? Just do it. Why are you bothering me with this? It's a simple task. Her father's tour is over, and they'll be heading back home next week. Just close it out and let me get back to these accounts."

"I wouldn't bother you with this if I didn't think it was important. I really think you should take a look at her passbook before I do anything."

"Why?"

"Just have a look."

"OK, fine. Give it to me.

"Oh, I see. You had better get Mr. Branson on the line for me."

"Hello?"

"Mr. Branson. This is George at the bank."

"Oh, hi, George. What's the problem? Did my wife forget to sign one of her checks again?"

"Oh no, Mr. Branson, nothing like that. It's Natalie. She just came in and wants to close out her account so, since she's only sixteen, I thought I should give you a call first."

"Is there a problem?"

"Well not technically, but she is only sixteen and--

"Look, George, she's been babysitting every night all summer—ever since school let out—getting home really late. She says even though she will only be a junior next year, she wants to get a head start on her college fund. She must have three or even four hundred dollars saved up by now. Undoubtedly she wants to shift it to her savings account back home."

"Uh, Mr. Branson?"

"Yes, George."

"I'll do whatever you want, but first I thought I should give you a call, as a courtesy mind you, to let you know that her balance is a little over $12,000," ($45,000 in 2014 dollars).

Long pause.

"Don't do anything and *please* don't mention this to anyone. I'll be there in fifteen minutes."

## Preliberal Times

Liberal thinking was not pervasive during this era, and the local Kwaj leaders believed part of their job was to safeguard the moral fiber and ethics of their community. The newspaper and local radio station both toed the line by restricting their local news to noncontroversial topics that seldom cast the army in an unflattering light.

Single males, prevented from what Mother Nature had intended them to pursue, will find a way—it's always been that way and always will be. The high moral standards reported in high school history books about our founding fathers were never as high as implied. It was all selective editing of history (a technique developed three days after writing was invented).

The site designers had decided that single women would not be permitted to work on site in order to head off potential problems. What was intended to be a prudent policy only exacerbated the situation and actually put the high school students at a greater risk of attracting too much attention to themselves from the bachelors.

## WHAT PROBLEM?

Most commanding officers (always colonels) on Kwajalein were treated courteously by the nonmilitary residents, but were not held in particularly high regard, with one exception. This colonel was not aloof and felt strongly that any situation that harmed no one should not be interfered with. Two months into his new command, he walked into the weekly meeting of his staff officers.

"What's the topic today, gentlemen?"

"Well sir, we are trying to figure out what to do about a newly discovered homosexual problem on Roi."

"What's the problem? Is there an odd number of them?"

Subject dropped. Problem became a nonproblem. Staff officers looked for a new problem to make themselves look busy and important.

## RUMOR

I have no direct verification of the following rumor, although I did hear it from two unrelated sources.

A Marshallese administrator handled the clearances of the Marshallese maids to assure they had background checks and were sufficiently trained to perform domestic duties on Kwajalein. He approved their applications and assigned identification badges. These badges were highly coveted, as they permitted the Marshallese to board the daily ferry from Ebeye to Kwaj for gainful employment. His position was unique, and he could easily have abused his authority to the maids' detriment. He knew all the young maids who might have been interested in earning a little extra income by providing comfort to some of the lonely bachelors. In summary, the rumor referred to the above-mentioned administrator as being a successful pimp.

If this prostitution rumor were true, it would have been in everyone's best interest to be as discrete as possible, which may have explained why so few nonbachelors were aware of it.

# 24

# SATO

Sato lived on Ebeye with his wife and three-year-old son, next door to his cherished father and mother; his was a particularly close family. His divinity college degree, earned in the States, gave him the credentials and respect to secure a position as an assistant minister on Ebeye. Although Sato was only in his midtwenties when I first met him, he was already well established in the Ebeye community and was admired for his education, wisdom, organization talents, humor, domestic counseling abilities, and the oratory skills displayed in his sermons.

I got to know Sato better than any of the other Marshallese on Ebeye, as he was our interpreter and guide on a ten-day, five-bachelor (all engineers) trip throughout the Marshall Islands on the *Louisa*, the ketch owned and captained by Felix DeBrum. On the long nights motoring between islands, we would talk late into the night about everything we could think of.

Years earlier he had accepted a scholarship to a divinity college, as it was the only game in town. The local Kwajalein churches were successful in raising funds to send protégés back for serious religious training, whereas most other education opportunities were severely limited.

## THE VANISHING WATCH

During our many outer-atoll excursion-planning meetings, the five of us realized that Sato did not sport a wristwatch. Figuring that a watch would be useful during our trip, we presented him with a diving watch a week prior to our departure. Later, after a few days at sea, we observed that he was not wearing his gift. We did not want to embarrass him by implying he had either lost his watch or forgotten to bring it on our trip, so we unceremoniously slipped him a replacement—one that we had originally purchased as a possible gift for one of the chiefs whose island we had hoped to visit.

Three islands and four days later, his wrist was bare once again. It was then we began to appreciate that the Marshallese custom of sharing was more engrained in their lifestyle than we thought.

Anytime someone of near-equal or higher status admired a possession, the possessor was obliged to offer it to them, and as often as not, the admirer did not hesitate to accept the offer.

As later explained to me by a Peace Corps teacher on Alinglaplap, "That watch you worried about will undoubtedly change hands several times during the next week and will eventually acquire the status of a community possession. Private property is mostly a Western concept, whereas, as with many other non-western cultures, community property is more the norm with the Marshallese. It's also possible this custom was reinforced during times of extreme deprivation when sharing was an essential tool for survival."

The third "watch for Sato" was not presented to him until our return home and then only after having it engraved, "To Sato, our good friend."

I do remember Sato wearing it a month later—a record for him—but then we lost touch, so I can't verify what happened to it after that.

## My Mother's Older Than Yours

Sato and I were talking as we strolled the beach on Namorik, about six days out, when two encounters occurred that gave me more insight into the workings of Marshallese society.

First we met a young man about two years older than Sato. The two of them were first cousins, and after initial greetings, they paused to chat for about fifteen minutes. I noticed that even though Sato was shorter and younger, his cousin assumed a very subservient posture.

Once we were out of earshot, Sato turned to me with a big smile and explained the encounter with, "My mother's older than his." As far as he was concerned, that was all the explanation he needed to give me.

Being a bit puzzled, I couldn't let it drop there.

Sato explained that the Marshallese practiced a matriarchal method of inheritance and power. Power is held by the men, but inherited though a mother's seniority. "Because my mother is older than my cousin's mother, I will inherit our family leadership, and he will have to be content with a lesser position."

## BOTH CUSTOMS

Sato did not retain his smugness for long. A little further down the beach we ran into an eleven-year-old girl. This time it was Sato who took an inferior posture.

After a brief conversation, we said our goodbyes and left her to continue down the beach. He looked awful, clearly shaken.

"What's wrong? Don't tell me her mother is also older than your mother."

"Oh no. Her father is the chief of this island and already has great power."

"What then?"

"She wanted to know all about my three-year-old son. She said she has heard he is very beautiful and very smart."

"That sounds like a compliment to me."

"Not really. I think she was working up the courage to admire him directly. If that happens, I might have to offer him to her. I love my son more than anything and couldn't bear to lose him."

I found out a few months later that Sato encountered this risk a few more times, until he came up with a brilliant solution. He gave his son to his father. His father was a senior member of the community and as such, would never be challenged over guardianship of Sato's son. Since the son spent most of his time at Grandpa's house anyway, all were content.

# 25

# EBEYE AND EBEYANS

It's the bright lights—the allure of the big city. The outer islands are idyllic, but once the restless young are exposed to the excitement and glamour of the big city, there's no way you can keep them back on the isle. It's the same historic city-migration pattern that has played out worldwide over the last couple hundred years. They want to be where the action is—where it's all happening.

When Japan assumed the administration of Kwajalein in 1914, Ebeye, the eighty-acre island three miles northeast of its larger neighbor, had a hundred residents at most.

After the Americans took control of the Marshall Islands toward the end of World War II, immigration swelled Ebeye's population quite dramatically due to increased job opportunities in support of several US military missions. These included World War II cleanup, military involvement in Asia, and the nuclear testing both at Bikini and Eniwetok.

The Bikini residents, evacuated from their island to accommodate the atomic bomb tests, were temporarily housed on Kwajalein, further straining the island's resources. The Bikini natives were eventually resettled on Kili, an uninhabited, lagoonless island to the south (an island I visited during my second tour in 1967). By the late 1950s, Ebeye's population had mushroomed to 1,500.

In the early 1960s, rising Cold War tensions pushed Congress to direct the Pentagon to establish a missile-reentry physics studies program. Kwajalein was chosen as an optimal downrange missile-reentry target location, as it was already under the US government's jurisdiction, was quite isolated, and had a sparse local population. The few Marshallese living in Kwajalein's midatoll corridor (those islands between Roi-Namur and Kwajalein) were evacuated and relocated to Ebeye, as errant missiles would pose a potential danger to anyone residing in the corridor. A missile mishap, in addition to being a tragedy, would have become a PR nightmare.

Kwajalein's expanding activities and corresponding thirst for a growing labor pool enticed even more Marshallese to migrate to Ebeye from the outer islands. Even after the demand for laborers subsided, the outer-island residents kept flooding to Ebeye—the big lifestyle magnet—where extended family members were already well established.

Both the Marshallese and the US Trust Territory governments became concerned that the burgeoning population growth, 1,500 in mid-1950s, 3,500 in 1965, 4,500 in 1966 (and by 2007 over 15,000, a population density greater than that of Manhattan) severely overtaxed Ebeye's limited resources. As such, both governments initiated programs to encourage nonessential Marshallese to return to their home islands. But, like the historic "Go west, young man, go west," the migration had taken on a life of its own—it could not be stopped.

## Jo-Jo

Jo-Jo was a Marshallese friend who often hung out at my friend Scott's trailer. One day while I was visiting Scott, Jo-Jo brought his cousin along.

"This is my cousin, Jim. He's been living on Ebeye even longer than me—almost fifteen years."

Jim was very affable, and after the usual five minutes of small talk, Jo-Jo volunteered, "Jim is a good welder and makes a lot of money. More money than almost anyone on Ebeye—except the king, of course."

After Jim left, Jo-Jo lingered to chat some more about his cousin. I asked, "If Jim makes so much money and Ebeye has no taxes (not introduced until a few years later), he must own his own house and live a good life."

Jo-Jo laughed, "Oh no. He rents and has no money."

"But how can that be?"

"Once his 'family' [translation: tribe or clan] learned that he lived in a big house and had a good job, many of them came to Ebeye and moved in with him."

"Oh really—and how many live with him now?"

"Seventeen, maybe eighteen relatives live with him—they come and go—and he's not even married and has no kids."

"Wow. Can't he ask some of them to go back home or move in with someone else?"

"No, no, never. He could never turn a relative away. He would lose face. It just isn't done."

"How many of these relatives have jobs?"

"Only him. Some look for work but, since Jim has a good income, they don't look very hard. No need."

The same tradition of sharing that enables mutual survival during harsh times handicaps saving and capital formation during good times.

## INTERISLAND ROMANCES

Most Kwajalein residents made a visit to Ebeye once or twice during their Kwaj tours, either out of curiosity or to pursue some sort of charity or religious endeavor. I averaged a trip to Ebeye every couple of months to see my Marshallese friend Sato, for a change of scenery, or even just to eat at the Ebeye Japanese restaurant. The Marshallese had retained their fondness for Japanese food.

A few Kwaj-ites, particularly bachelors, visited this island nearly every weekend. My guess is that a good two dozen Kwaj bachelors had permanent girlfriends on Ebeye (including one married friend in a trailer near mine). A few young couples were either living together or were actually married. They kept a low profile, as the army was particularly sensitive about local fraternization and didn't want to risk any bad press (it's always about PR).

## WELL MEANING—MOSTLY WRONG

The young, idealistic Peace Corps volunteer was eager to make her contribution to the world, a worthwhile and admirable goal that we all would applaud. After landing on Kwajalein, she took the ferry to Ebeye with several of her covolunteers to await further transport to her assigned remote island and to begin her adventure.

This was her first actual exposure to any form of Marshallese culture, and she was appalled by what she found on Ebeye. She was met with serious overcrowding, substandard sanitation, numerous Western trappings (e.g., bad diets and smoking), and a paucity of vegetation except for a few token palm trees.

When she finally reached her new home on one of the more re- mote atolls to begin her two-year stint, she found an environment much more in tune with what she had anticipated. The contrast between her Ebeye experience and her new home-island environ- ment was too much for her sensibilities. She felt compelled to write a rather unflattering article for her hometown paper. She elaborated on how awful the American officials had behaved when they forced so many Marshallese to remain on an island as small as Ebeye, while many of the outer islands were paradise-like and sparsely populated. She was particularly upset by how the "Americans" had bulldozed so much of the Ebeye vegetation into the lagoon and replaced the natural growth with concrete.

This idealistic, well-meaning volunteer was poorly informed and relied only on her eyes and emotions to reach her conclusions, instead of researching the actual facts. It was the Japanese who had bulldozed Ebeye to construct their seaplane base during their final preparation for World War II, while the Americans, after gaining control from the Japanese, constructed housing, replanted, and generally restored much of the island. She also never understood that the Marshallese did not want to go home—Ebeye was where the young, typically 50 percent of the population, preferred to live.

The one element of truth in her assessment, however, was that the Americans did exacerbate the overcrowding with their labor requirements, which arose from their support for the nuclear bomb tests, the Asian conflicts, and their missile-reentry research programs—all activities driven by the pressures of the Cold War.

A few other local newspapers picked up her unfavorable arti- cle, but as Kwajalein was in the middle of nowhere, its impact was short lived.

## The Lease

The following is not firsthand knowledge, but it does represent a consensus of what expats living on Kwajalein *believed* during my tours there.

When the US government wished to enter into negotiations to lease portions of the Kwajalein Atoll, they were stymied by the question of with whom they should negotiate. Who was in power? Who owned what? Who had control? What were the local ground rules?

The Marshallese concept of ownership/land control was nearly unfathomable to Americans, who were used to their own English-based understanding of the topic. The American negotiators soon discovered there were numerous kings and chiefs who held fractional interests in the various properties the United States wished to lease, even though some of these individuals lived on remote islands.

As the US officials were under pressure to "get this thing done," they finally resorted to a highly creative and proactive approach.

They picked one high-profile king, King Kabua, who appeared to have a considerable amount of authority. They negotiated with King Kabua and his advisors with the understanding that, "We are negotiating with you, but how that will affect the other kings and people in power is up to all of you to figure out." It was even possible that King Kabua was not the most senior Marshallese king, but rather just the most available. The US government avoided getting involved in the detailed wranglings that might have occurred among the Marshallese who had vested interests in the leased islands. "It's their problem and their job to figure it all out." In any event, the US government secured an agreement that included leasing eleven of the ninety-six Kwajalein Atoll islands.

Side note—for security reasons, all Marshallese visiting Kwajalein for work or just to visit were required to wear badges listing their name and job description. I observed one day, when King Kabua disembarked the Ebeye-Kwajalein commute ferry from Ebeye, that he too had his job description on his badge—"King."

# 26

# HIDDEN POWER

## REAL POWER MAY NOT BE WHERE YOU EXPECT IT

During my first tour, I was responsible for the electronics portion of the operation. This involved the maintenance and upgrading of remote optical sensors, including three tracking cameras located on three separate islands and a 48" slewing spectrograph telescope on Roi—all controlled by our IBM 7090 mainframe computer on Roi-Namur. The three tracking cameras gathered data that were used post-mission to triangulate very precise trajectory measurements of the test missile and any light-emitting decoys during reentry.

In those days, tracking missiles with radars was not as accurate as using optical triangulation, so Central Mission Command would not permit launches until all optical cameras were "up" (fully operational, referred to as "green" status).

One statistically unlucky day while we were preparing for a 9:00 p.m. launch, all three tracking cameras went down—each for a different reason. I repaired camera number one on Roi-Namur, then returned to Kwajalein in order to catch the 3:00 p.m. commuter boat to Ennylabegan to work on camera number two. If all went well, I could just catch the last shuttle boat at 5:00 p.m. to reach Kwajalein in time to repair camera number three without impacting the mission schedule. I don't know the actual cost per hour hold of a mission, but if the personnel (all on overtime) in California, Hawaii, and Kwajalein were factored in, it had to be in the several-hundred-thousand-dollars-per-hour range.

On the way over, the two boat operators were rather cocky and concluded that I, their only passenger, was a rather low-level lackey of minimal importance.

They shouted to me over the engine noise, "We're probably going to get out of here fifteen minutes early. It's our last run of the day and we want to get back. Be here at 4:40 or you might have to spend the night."

"Can't guarantee that. You're going to have to wait for me until at least five. That is the scheduled departure isn't it? It's very important to tonight's mission that I get back to Kwajalein after I finish my work here."

Their nod was more like a dismissal than agreement. I didn't have much confidence that they took me seriously, so I repeated.

"It's critical that you not leave without me."

I managed to complete the repair by a quarter of five and rushed back down to the pier. I arrived at ten to—in plenty of time. The boatmen did not wait and had just pulled away. No amount of waving and yelling would encourage them to turn back, even though I saw them point back in my direction and laugh. They were smug and probably talked among themselves: "I guess we showed him. Demanding we wait. Just who the f*** does he think he is? We're not going to take any sh** from that a**hole. Next time he'll do it our way or we'll leave him again."

Wrong decision.

I called my supervisor and explained my predicament and its probable impact to the mission.

"I got back to the pier on time but they took off early, even after I had strongly requested they wait. I tried to impress upon them the importance of my getting back to Kwaj in time to finish some crucial repairs crucial for tonight's mission. They saw me waving from the pier but ignored me. They were a pretty cocky pair. What do you suggest?"

"Bad move on their part. I'll see what I can do."

He called our site manager to apprise him of the situation. Our site manager then contacted the commanding officer to explain just how serious this problem could become if not resolved. The commanding officer, who wished to avoid an expensive delay as well as making the Kwajalein command look bad, immediately dispatched his personal official speedboat to pick me up. I arrived on Kwajalein in time to repair the third camera without having to request an expensive mission hold.

Two weeks later I had to take the commuter boat once again to Ennylabegan for some camera-modification work. The same two guys were operating the boat. This time they looked rather sheepish and, amazingly, treated me with considerable deference. They seemed downright humble.

They had been severely reprimanded for "teaching me a lesson." They were lectured as to how they had jeopardized a high-profile mission by violating the rules and leaving a very mission-critical scientist behind. They were put on a very short probationary leash and told they were less than an eyelash away from being fired and shipped home. Now they were bending over backward to ensure that I was a happy camper on my second trip. They pushed off for the return trip precisely at five. I suspect they would have waited all night for me, had I asked.

## NOT OPENING THE DINING HALL

An eight-hour radar-calibration countdown procedure was required to obtain optimal data quality for each reentry test. The final three hours of this process had to be performed continuously without a break. Tests usually occurred around nine o'clock, so essential personnel would have to return from dinner no later than six o'clock.

One mission, however, had an unusual launch location and altered configuration that required an earlier mission start time. This change meant the mess hall needed to be opened an hour earlier than usual to accommodate the standard calibration sequence.

The contractor's logistics manager on Roi-Namur refused to accommodate our request.

"Can't do that. It's not in our contract, and I have no authority to alter our mess hall schedule."

No amount of cajoling or persuasion had any effect on getting him to alter his stance. His actual motivation, not disclosed at the time, was that he would have had to pay four kitchen workers over-time. As his bonus was based on keeping overtime to a minimum, his self-interest was in direct conflict with the missile range's inter-est. The potential $150 saved by the contractor by not  the kitchen staff overtime was minuscule compared to the cost of an hour hold to the mission overall.

Roi-Namur TRADEX (name of main radar) operations to com-mand: "We are requesting an hour hold on this mission."

"Hold granted. Tell me though, how can you possibly call an hour hold so long before launch?"

"We are unable to persuade the contractor on Roi to open the mess hall for our staff an hour early."

"WHAT??"

Click.

One minute later the phone rings.

"We'd be only too happy to open the mess hall an hour early for you. If there is any other way we can be of assistance to you, please do not hesitate to ask."

# 27

# PEACE CORPS STORIES

When the Peace Corps was expanded to service the US Trust Territory, this entire North Pacific area had a population on the order of one hundred thousand. Ironically, the one thousand volunteers trained and assigned throughout the territory increased the territory's population by 1 percent.

The most prophetic statement in the speeches greeting the newly arrived Peace Corps volunteers was, "This program spells the beginning of the end of the power of the interpreters."

A few years later, while on a ten-day *Louisa* charter cruise to several outer islands with four friends, I met several of these Peace Corps volunteers in their working/teaching environments and enjoyed hearing their stories firsthand.

After we gained permission from the headman to make landfall onto each island, we would start our forays by distributing gifts, more of the token variety rather than anything of real value. Fishing hooks, bubble gum, candy, and cigarettes were some of the more popular offerings. We reserved the more valuable items to trade for handicrafts, shells, and other souvenirs during our short visits—usually a day or two on each island.

When offered cigarettes, one young man in his early twenties on Ailingalaplap presented us with the most reverent countenance he could muster and responded, with his hand held up in denial, "Oh, no thank you. I'm a Christian." A few minutes later, after the crowds dispersed, he returned with, "Actually my friend smokes so, if you don't mind, I'll take some cigarettes for him."

Later a young resident Peace Corps volunteer translated this little theater for me: "I'd love some cigarettes, but with all these people watching, I have to present my 'Good Christian' face and turn them down. Now that no one's here to see me—yes, please, I'd really like some."

"He'll smoke them in the *binjo* [outhouse] when no one's watching and share a few with his other 'Good Christian' buddies."

Another motivation for his wanting cigarettes was that in these remote islands, cigarettes often served as a second currency that helped keep the local commerce moving.

On Namorik, I met Heather and Carl, a young married couple sent by the Peace Corps to establish a grade-one-through-eight school. As they proudly showed me around their new home, they related several very interesting stories that gave me some insight into the workings of the local Marshallese culture.

"A few months after we came here, we learned that on *day one*, a group of Marshallese youths made a running bet as to which one of us would be seduced first. I'm afraid we've been a big disappointment to them in this endeavor.

"We didn't fully appreciate how 'active' the young people were until the morning we arrived at the school a half hour early. We found two eighth graders going at it behind our desk.

"With no television, no cars, and privacy at a premium, I guess we should have been surprised it happened only once."

One evening the council met to take up Heather and Carl's proposal that a 10:00 p.m. curfew be set for all children under fourteen.

"We've been teaching your children for two months now and are happy to tell you how smart they all are. Mornings are fine, but by the afternoons they are too tired to follow any of the instructions—they fall asleep at their desks.

"Your children are not getting enough sleep—they're staying up well past midnight. A curfew would help solve this problem. More sleep means better learning."

The proposal was discussed at great length, with everyone contributing except for one elder, Tom, who sat in the corner and listened with what appeared to be a fixed look of amusement on his face. All participants seemed to be in agreement that a vote in favor of a curfew made total sense—it was the right thing to do. But then just before the vote was taken, a senior member of the council turned to Tom and commented, "Tom, you've been listening to all our discussions and arguments but haven't spoken a word—that's not like you. Before we vote on this new rule, we all want to hear your opinion."

"The cause is an admirable one," Tom started off. "We all want the very best for the next generation, as it is so important to all our futures. And yes, we could vote to enact a ten o'clock curfew for all children under fourteen. Yes, we could do this."

He paused and then added, "I would like to point out, however, two years ago we prohibited adultery."

Everyone broke out laughing hysterically. The meeting never officially ended. The vote was never taken. All left still chuckling. Heather and Carl never brought the subject up again.

# 28

# MARSHALLESE STUDY GROUP

When I took over as the head of the Marshallese Study Group, an informal local club for expats wishing to increase their understanding of the local culture, I reorganized it to my liking—minimum bureaucracy. No membership lists, no dues, virtually no board meetings—only speakers and topics of interest. It was easier to pay the twenty-dollar monthly expenses out-of-pocket than worry about raising funds from the few dozen members.

Our most interesting speaker was Dwight Heine, the first Marshallese native to earn a baccalaureate from the University of Hawaii (in 1959), the first Marshallese to serve as district administrator of the Trust Territory, and later one of the four "Great Marshallese" honored by a commemorative stamp issued in 2001.

One benefit I enjoyed for making the study group's program arrangements was the honor of hosting each speaker for dinner at home prior to their presentation. Dwight's private dinner stories were by far the most memorable. Two of my favorites that he shared with me that spring evening in 1967 follow below.

## CAPTURED JAPANESE FLAGS

I [Dwight Heine] was only a teenager when the battle for Kwajalein took place in February 1944. I hung around the base most days after the US Army secured the island, mostly out of curiosity and for something to do. I tried to make myself as useful as I could so they would let me stay. As a result, I made many friends with the American soldiers stationed here, several of whom were not much older than I was.

A couple of my cousins and I soon figured out that these GIs were hungry for souvenirs of the Pacific conflict—any kind of souvenirs they could send home. Within a few months, we had a thriving business supplying the GIs with "authentic" captured Japanese flags displaying the Rising Sun surrounded by genuine Japanese writing. They never did realize that the raw materials for these "authentic" flags were sheets "borrowed" from the army hospital and decorated to look as official as possible given our limited resources. We had a real problem keeping up with demand.

We couldn't help but add a little private joke to our creations. Remember, we were only teenagers and did what teenagers do. If someone had actually translated the Japanese characters we put on these flags, they would have read, "There's a sucker born every minute."

## THIRD-CLASS TRANSLATOR

I [Dwight Heine] was considered one of the good guys after the Americans took over control of Kwajalein, for in my small way, I had helped the Americans gather intelligence before the invasion. [Dwight didn't elaborate on the details of this contribution.] One of the officers in charge looked for some way to find me a paying job. I had picked up a little English from hanging around with the American soldiers for several months—not enough to communicate well, but I was better at it than any of my cousins—meaning I could fake it better than they could.

Fortunately for me, the army was desperate for translators at any skill level, so they gave me a job with a title. I was officially a third-class translator. I think they may have invented this title, for I never ran across another third-class translator—I was it. After a few months at my new job, mostly with noncommissioned officers, I actually improved to the point where I could handle most of my assignments without help and without screwing up too much.

But then one day, the admiral, the important guy with all that stuff on his uniform, arrived unexpectedly and requested a first-class translator. He wished to visit several of the outer islands on a goodwill tour to learn firsthand how the Marshallese natives viewed the Americans taking over control from the Japanese.

To his disappointment, all the first-class translators and even the second-class translators were occupied off island and would not be available for several days.

The local command was in a quandary. The admiral could not wait, so if he were to make the journey at all, he would have to make do with a less-skilled translator. They knew I was nowhere near qualified to translate for a high-ranking officer—particularly the admiral. Nonetheless, the admiral decided to take a chance on me—and hoped for the best.

Our first stop was Majuro, the most important Marshallese island after Kwajalein. I had a large number of friends and relatives on Majuro, so I knew they would go along with anything I said in my translation.

On our way to Majuro, I overheard the admiral lecture his entourage about his philosophy on how to give a good speech in an unfamiliar environment. He explained it was always helpful to begin a speech with a joke to break the ice—to show he was human and not all business. He had honed this technique over his many years with the navy and found it quite successful—although lately, he complained, some of the translators in this Pacific region had messed it up for him.

Upon our arrival, we were greeted by the chief and his committee of the more important island elders. After I translated their brief greetings for the admiral and his entourage, refreshments were served; we were then led to the island's meeting ground, where most of the island populace had assembled awaiting our arrival. The chief spoke first, explaining how things were changing now that the fighting in the Marshall Islands was over. The Japanese had been driven out and the US authorities were now in control. He finished his introduction by describing what he thought the admiral hoped to achieve by this visit.

Then it was the admiral's turn. He greeted the crowd with the Marshallese aloha-like greeting, "Yokwe yuk," smiled, and in full voice began his joke, which, fortunately, I had heard him practice on the way over.

When he finished, he paused, looked at me with a bit of apprehension, and awaited my translation.

"Friends and relatives. I will stall for a bit and try to match the length of my talking to the length of the admiral's introduction to make it appear that I am actually translating what he just said. The admiral has just told his favorite joke. This joke is very funny in his culture but is not funny at all in our culture. So to be polite, you will now all please laugh."

The Marshallese all thought this was hilarious and laughed until their sides began to hurt.

The admiral beamed and commented to his aide, "Finally! A translator who got it right!"

"I," Dwight concluded his story triumphantly, "left Kwajalein a third-class translator but returned a first-class translator."

# 29

# GAMBLING

Most of the gambling on Kwajalein, except for football numbers, was confined to the bachelor world, so I have limited firsthand knowledge—only the rumors that made the rounds.

## BOB

Bob was addicted to poker but, unfortunately, was not very good at it. When not playing cards, he worked three jobs to satisfy his gambling creditors, who were content to leave him well enough alone as long as he paid them a good portion of his income on a regular basis. They had a good thing going—he did not. They instinctively followed the Laffer curve (popularized by Arthur Laffer to explain the relationship between taxation rates and total revenue) which allowed him to keep just enough of his wages to enjoy a few luxuries while on Kwaj but not enough for him to get out of debt. The consortium of bachelors to which he owed so much money had not permitted him to take a vacation for nearly three years lest, once off island, he'd disappear altogether. Finally, pushed by his boss's insistence that he take a vacation, they acquiesced and let him go to Hawaii for three weeks, but only if he followed strict guidelines. Their Hawaiian associates kept close tabs on him during his whole stay.

## JIM

Jim had been kicked off island only a few months after his arrival. He was caught drinking on the job a third time after being warned of the consequences. This posed a quandary to the runner of that week's football pool, as Jim had won $100,000 (in 1967 dollars) two days after his hasty departure. He eventually did receive his winnings.

## JAB

There was one high-stakes Asian gambling game that required a large amount of cash to facilitate its operation. To this end, a $25,000 "bank" was kept in a paper bag inside an organizer's footlocker in his room. This worked quite well for years, until one day the funds used to bank the game went "poof."

Since gambling was strictly against island rules, no one wanted to jeopardize its operation or their jobs, so the theft went unreported.

Coincidently, one of the frequent participants was found dead a week later. As was standard procedure in crimes of this severity, detectives from Honolulu were brought in to handle the investigation. A few days later, they left after concluding the man's death was suicide by hanging. The official explanation was the man was depressed, put a noose around his neck, and jumped from his bunk. Most residents didn't buy this explanation, since he apparently jumped from the lower bunk.

A few months after the fuss blew over, the game resumed, and to my knowledge, the "bank" never went missing after that.

## CHARITY FAIR

Once a year the island pulled together and organized the Kwajalein Charity Fair to raise funds for various local charities supported by the Kwajalein residents. There were over sixty different booths in all, running full tilt over the fair's weekend of activity. It proved a bit awkward for the local command when they learned that well over 50 percent of the funds raised at the entire fair came from a single booth, the Lincoln Lab's gambling booth. This game involved the operator throwing three dice while the participants bet on the sum total of all three dice. The odds for each possible outcome are easy calculations (e.g., 216 to 1 for a sum of 3) but like roulette in Vegas, the actual payback was shaved to give the house a long-term advantage (e.g., paying only 200 to 1 to the winner on a bet of a sum of 3). The bachelors crowded the booth endlessly, placing the maximum bets allowed while the scientists and engineers, experts in probability, stayed away. All the pent-up gambling desire of these bachelors (reinforced by pockets full of cash) was unleashed—and legally too (all for a good cause). Tempers flared and gamblers got a bit hot under the collar, but no fights broke out, and very little drunkenness was reported. In the end, it all worked out without embarrassing the local command, and the charity fair raised considerably more than expected.

# 30

# ESCAPE ARTIST

Nearly every engineer who has ever worked for a medium-sized company has run across at least one "Jerry" in his life. He's the guy who always seems to dodge the silver bullet; he obscures the fact that he is incompetent in his professed field, liberally borrows from other people's work, blows lots of smoke, and adopts the right vocabulary to obscure his shortcomings. Eventually these "Jerrys" are unmasked, but not before they've milked their position to their advantage and to their employer's detriment. Just prior to getting axed, they are usually able to implement a successful escape plan—"to a better job."

The Jerrys I knew weren't dumb. They played their professed role as "expert" to the hilt, while in truth, they were nowhere near up to snuff as advertised. The one I knew on Kwajalein had been laid off at Perkin-Elmer after he had overextended his charade. He heard that MIT Lincoln Lab was ramping up a reentry-study program for the army, utilizing advanced optics and state-of-the-art electronics. He applied for and obtained a job interview.

Initially he intended to pass himself off as an electronics expert but quickly discovered Lincoln Lab was the home of some of the top electronics personnel in the country—so no hope there. However, he quickly realized they were babes in the woods when it came to optics, so mid-interview, he switched his pitch to sell himself as an optics expert—he got the job.

In the beginning Jerry managed to cover up his inadequacies as head of the Kwajalein optics operations by relying heavily on the work of others and by making sure all reports produced by his underlings passed through him.

Result? The MIT personnel bragged that they had successfully hired Jerry away from a high-level prestigious position at Perkin-Elmer, not realizing that he was actually in the process of being fired for incompetence.

Craig, on the other hand, was Jerry's opposite. Where Jerry was savvy, but lacked technical skills, Craig was technically strong but naive in dealing with the real world.

When Craig graduated in ancient Greek studies from Harvard, he stood, diploma in hand, with no idea of what to do next. He thought, "Where is the government guy or the Harvard representative to tell me where to go for my job?"

He told me when we were on Kwajalein, six years after his graduation, that he really had believed that if you studied hard and got all As at Harvard, the system would provide you with a job without any effort on your part.

Finally, (and only because he had taken an astronomy course on a whim his senior year) Craig secured a job teaching astronomy to high school students at the Smithsonian Astronomical Observatory in Washington—pay: minimum wage. His astronomy experience ultimately led to his job processing optical-tracking data of missile reentries using triangulation algorithms.

Craig thrived at his new job and spent his spare time scouring any literature he could find on the subject. He independently developed new algorithms to achieve greatly improved levels of accuracy in determining reentry trajectories from the recorded optical data. As head of the department, Jerry took total credit for this breakthrough, and when the powers that be asked Jerry to write a report on the new techniques, he of course assigned Craig the job.

"Craig, our guys back at the lab are very impressed by the improved optical-tracking results you've been sending them these last few months."

"Really? I wasn't sure anyone noticed."

"Of course they noticed. I told them in great detail how hard you've been working in your spare time to develop these new algorithms. They're definitely impressed and will certainly keep it in mind at review time."

"Wow! Finally someone appreciates my work. Did you tell them all about the improvement-measuring approaches I showed you?"

"Every bit of it. They asked me to pass on to you that your results actually exceed anything they thought possible.

"These guys would really like a detailed report on all the stuff you developed to achieve these breakthroughs. Think you could knock it out for them in three months?"

"I'll do my best. And thank you for supporting me in this."

Three months later, after long hours, evenings, and weekends, Craig submitted his hefty report to Jerry for approval.

Jerry did not understand a word of Craig's report, so he did the next-best thing. Without informing Craig, Jerry added his name to the 150-page report as principle investigator and passed it off as his own work. He told his superiors that he allowed Craig to add his name below, as Craig did contribute a few of the details and helped with the drawings.

When Craig asked what happened to his report, Jerry stonewalled him, saying it was in review back at the Lab's headquarters and would probably take several months to complete. It was six months before Craig learned the truth, by which time Jerry had disappeared.

When Jerry got wind that his charade had been uncovered and he was about to be let go, he once again implemented his proven escape strategy. A very happy recruiter at one of MIT's competitors was convinced he pulled off a real coup, stealing MIT's top optics expert, not realizing Jerry was just about to be history anyway. For what Jerry lacked in technical skills, he more than made up with his escape-artist savvy.

One can't help but wonder if the higher he got, the more tenuous his position would become, unless of course he ran for public office.

More Macho Man—Not (See end of chapter 19)

Atlen, a similar-type character, was fresh from the mainland, where he too had conned MIT into believing he was an optics expert and had successfully convinced his new boss on Kwaj (not Jerry) that he could do almost anything. A few weeks after his arrival, his boss sent him up a 24-foot ladder on the exterior of the telescope dome to perform some routine maintenance on the doors shielding the large, 48-inch telescope. No one saw Atlen the rest of the day until late afternoon, when he was discovered white-knuckled, two-thirds of the way up the ladder. Atlen suffered from severe acrophobia and had failed to inform anyone of this minor handicap.

However, the final straw came during his third month on site. Atlen, a self-proclaimed optics expert, was asked to clean the 48-inch, delicate, silvered lens. Anyone working with large telescopes (at least during the sixties) knew that lens cleaning involved using a super soft cloth (e.g., an old cotton T-shirt) with the mildest of soaps and warm water to very gingerly wash the surface. Even using a tissue or a paper towel would scratch the delicate lens.

Atlen was fired on the spot when he was discovered scrubbing the lens with Clorox, irreparably damaging the reflective silvering, completely degrading the several-hundred-thousand-dollar lens.

# 31

# RAYMOND

Every morning Raymond would fly from Kwajalein to Roi-Namur like most of the MIT staff. He'd take care of the normal paperwork and oversee the Roi-Namur optical installation from morning through early afternoon. Midafternoon he'd take the 3:00 p.m. flight back to check on the one optical site located on Kwajalein Island itself to make sure scheduled maintenance, mission preparations, and needed repairs were all taken care of.

Raymond was aware that the three-man crew that worked the Kwajalein site had a tendency to slack off if they could get away with it, so he called the Kwajalein site every morning to check on them as soon as he reached his Roi office.

"Hello, Kwaj optics, Tom here."

"Tom. Tell me what's happening."

"Sure, Raymond. I'm cleaning up the debris left over from last Friday's test. George is up running a diagnostic on the repeater—it had a few glitches last mission. He may have to replace some 2N708 transistors. Oh, and Mike is redoing the tool bench and inventorying the spares like you asked him to."

"So everyone is there then?"

"Yup, not a problem. I may need to make a run to pick up some light bulbs later, but other than that, we'll be here all day."

This routine was played out in various forms each morning for six months, and Raymond was satisfied that his Kwaj workers were seldom late, although he did suspect they covered for each other once in a while if one of them did not make it in on time. One day Raymond unexpectedly missed his flight to Roi, so he decided to drop by the Kwaj site himself while he waited for the 9:00 a.m. flight rather than call in later from Roi.

Upon his arrival, he was surprised to find the doors locked and the station abandoned. He waited a full hour and still no one showed, so he decided to skip the 9:00 a.m. flight. On a hunch, he called the number he usually called when checking in from the seldom-used backup phone.

Staring at the unattended but now ringing phone in front of him he heard, "Hi, Kwaj optical site."

"Tom. Sorry I couldn't call earlier. How's everyone doing this morning?"

"Everything's fine. I wondered why you hadn't called earlier. We've all been here since eight. George just left to get another reel of #14 copper wire and Mike is restocking the 2N708s that just arrived. We were down to barely a dozen, and as you know, they're our workhorse transistors."

Raymond felt strange listening to someone supposedly talk on the unattended phone, but he continued his subterfuge. No sense giving it away that he was onto them—at least not just yet.

"Fine. Tell George I need to talk to him so I'll call back in an hour."

Raymond made a cup of coffee and waited. An hour later he called the primary number again and got George on the line.

"Any problem securing the #14 wire?"

"No—they were fully stocked."

"OK, thanks."

Raymond then called Personnel, explained the situation, and said he was going over to their quarters. He asked Personnel to call the optics phone number in fifteen minutes, at which time Raymond would be knocking on their door.

The three were astonished to find Raymond at their door as they professed to Personnel that they were at the optical station.

Explanation—through their connections with the phone guy (everyone on Kwaj had connections; trading favors was like a second currency), they had an extension of the optic station phone installed in their room. Each morning they would take turns answering Raymond's call. Upon confrontation, they admitted that they seldom showed up to the site before noon. Two months later, they were history.

# 32

# GLASS BALLS

The residents of Kwajalein loved to collect souvenirs to forever remind them of their exotic life on Kwaj, that little piece of paradise in the middle of the Pacific. High on everyone's list were seashells, black coral, local carvings, storyboards, diving salvage, handicrafts, and my favorite, Japanese glass balls, a.k.a. Japanese fishing floats. There are clubs all around the world dedicated to collecting glass balls.

Norwegians produced the first glass floats in the 1840s to replace cork and wood floats in their gill nets. The Japanese adopted the technology around 1910, as these floats were ideal for their large deep-sea fishing industry, where strings of nets could reach up to fifty miles.

The balls were initially hand blown (some from recycled sake bottles, hence their green color) but were later blown into wooden molds to speed up the process. Fishermen would tie/weave a rope net (80 to 120 knots) tightly around each glass ball, which was then secured to the top floating edge of a fishingnet.

These floats have since been replaced with floats made out of plastic, Styrofoam, or even aluminum.

When the nets were hauled in, many of these floats either worked themselves loose or were cut free to set off on their multi-year, several-thousand-mile ocean odyssey driven by currents and winds. They tended to get captured in an endless circulating currents until a storm broke them away and they washed up onto a beach. The most prevalent landfalls were on the beaches of North America and the Pacific Islands.

The larger floats are of the sixteen-inch-diameter variety, while the smaller ones tend to have diameters around four inches. Most floats found on beaches are at least ten years old.

In my five years as an active beachcomber, I found only two floats on Roi-Namur during my lunch breaks and none on Kwaj—too much competition from avid early rising collectors. I was able to acquire a couple dozen off beaches (with permission from the locals) while visiting a few of the outer islands, and I traded for another twenty while on Kwajalein. I purchased the bulk of my hoard, at least a hundred, over the length of my last tour from Marshallese at $1.25 each in 1968. I gave away a couple dozen, sold as many for ten dollars each, and had close to a hundred stolen from the crawlspace under a rental, leaving me with only about twenty. Large glass balls with rope now retail for between $125 and $350.

## TRASH OR TREASURE? (A TRUE STORY)

"Tom, I hate it when I see the Marshallese picking through our Dumpster looking for stuff. They should pass a rule prohibiting this behavior. It's just so tacky."

"Sara, leave 'em alone. They're not doing any harm, and in a sense, they are actually helping. Think of it as recycling."

"Well. It's just not right and certainly not to the standards one would expect on a military installation. I'm going to talk to Marlene. Her husband is a captain and should be able to put a word in for me on this with the colonel."

A month later, Tom and Sara joined five other couples who had been invited to spend two days visiting a small Marshallese village on a neighboring island. They were hosted by a group of Marshallese families as arranged by the local Kwaj church to increase cross-cultural understanding.

"Tom, look at all those glass balls. There must be twenty of them. They're all in perfect condition. What do you think they're going to do with them?"

"Where?"

"Over there, behind those trees to the left of the path."

"Oh. That's their dump. They clean the whole island once a week, particularly the path down the center of the island and anything that may have washed up on shore. Then they just pile it up in their dump."

"Dump? They can't throw glass balls away. They're too valuable, too hard to find!"

"Well, that's what they do."

"Tom, since we're leaving tonight, do you think they would notice if we just took a few after dark?"

## IF HENNY PENNY COLLECTED GLASS BALLS

One of the outer islands I visited during my ten-day excursion had miles of long and very narrow shoreline with very limited area supporting a population of less than one hundred. They had so many glass balls on their shores, it almost looked like litter—too many for them to even bother gathering up.

I asked the headman, "Would it be all right for me to collect a dozen or so glass balls to bring home with me?"

"Why yes, of course—we have no use for them. Take as many as you wish."

I then polled my shipmates to see if they too wanted to gather a few as there were plenty for everyone. No one was interested—in fact, they couldn't understand why I was. So I spent a couple of hours by myself gathering and loading thirty of them onto our ship. I left at least a hundred on the beach.

Family and friends met us upon our return to Kwaj a week later. Several of my compatriots' wives eyed my small hoard. Then two of my shipmates approached me with, "when are we going to divide the glass balls?"

I was not as severe as Henny Penny in the baked-bread nursery rhyme story, even though I had every right to be. I gave two glass balls to each couple and kept the rest. That seemed to placate everyone.

## IMPORTING GLASS BALLS

Since I was a bachelor during my third and final tour, I had extra time on my hands and saw an opportunity to import glass balls back home, as they were worth $10 to $20 stateside at that time and I could buy ten a week for $1.25 a piece on Kwajalein.

First I sent four of them to an associate's sister in San Francisco who thought she could market them for me. A few months later I received a letter from her: "Success! Disney is very interested and the price is right. They want you to ship a minimum of ten thousand a week. Is that a problem?"

**Japanese fishing floats (a.k.a. glass balls)**

# 33

# SECURITY?

"Is everyone here? Could you secure the door please?"

Only three hundred people in the world had this particular high level of secret clearance, and of them, twenty-five were in that most inner-inner secure room in a top-secret, secure building on the secure island of Roi-Namur. Voices were hushed even though the room was soundproof, radio proof, and just-about-everything-else proof. The topic had such serious ramifications that the participants automatically lowered their voices.

The site manager began, "We just received a top-secret communiqué from stateside that the Chinese are about to launch their first satellite. Because we have the highest state-of-the-art collection of radars anywhere in the world, and we are on the direct flight path of the launch vehicle, we have been tasked with scanning the last stage and its payload to obtain as much data on this launch as possible.

"It's ninety percent probable that the launch will occur this Friday at eight in the evening. You should call home and cancel any social obligations you might have using the cover story that we need to reserve that timeslot for some special interference tests. Under no circumstances should you even allude to the nature of the actual exercise."

After fielding a few specific questions from the participants about which sensors would be employed and what manning levels would be needed, management reiterated the absolute importance that no word of this exercise be leaked. Then we were excused.

"Hello. Hi. I've just been informed we are going to run some very important interference tests Friday, so we'll need to cancel bridge with the Browns."

"No we don't."

"Ah, yes, we do. I can't go into the details now. It will have to wait until I get home."

"I tell you we don't have to cancel our plans. The Chinese have delayed their launch for at least a week."

I was still sitting stunned at my desk trying to absorb what had just transpired when the intercom requested that we reassemble in the inner-inner super-duper-secret room.

Before I could speak to anyone about my conversation, we were told again in a hushed voice, "We have just received an update that the Chinese have delayed their launch for at least a week, so you can continue with your previous social plans. Any questions?"

Before I could speak up, my officemate volunteered, "Uh, yeah. I just got off the phone with my wife, and she already briefed me about the delay."

A few others in the room confirmed similar experiences. Management was stunned.

The wives were all aware of our top-secret goings-on before our top brass were.

So where was the security leak?

A couple of days later, it all came out. The security leak was, as every wife on the island could have told you, the Kwajalein hairdresser. She knew everything before our fearless leaders did (although she had no idea that what she had unintentionally pieced together was classified). Or as one friend summed up, "If the hairdresser doesn't know it—it didn't happen." This was an inherent security problem that the *male* designers of our security installation had totally overlooked.

Project security came up with a very creative solution to this unforeseen problem. From that day on, all hairdressers working on Kwaj were required to have a top-secret clearance, including extensive background checks.

# 34

# JUST BEING HELPFUL

## (Yeah, Right!)

"I'm looking for the manager of the Crossroads Club. Is he around?"

"You're speaking to him. Are you Mr. Branson, by any chance?"

"That's right. Andy Branson."

"I'm delighted you came. I'm Clayton Lambert, but just call me Clay. I run the Bachelors' Club here and fill in as the sometime barkeep."

"My technician, Chuck, said you wanted to see me about our possibly upgrading your entertainment center in your club, or something like that."

"Yeah, Chuck is a regular. I got talking with him a few nights ago about this thing we just got, called a VHS tape machine. Problem is we don't know how to use it or even how to set it up. We're hoping you or someone you know can help. Chuck raves about you guys from Lincoln Lab and brags about how lucky he is to be working with such world class microwave engineers."

"He probably told you that after too many beers, and after we gave him a pretty hefty raise last week. That can go to a guy's head. But yes, we can help you. All we need from you is where you want it set up and a time you can give us unlimited access for a few hours."

"I can show you where it needs to go. It has to be placed where it can't be viewed by anyone outside the club, especially minors or we could get in trouble—remember, these are lonely bachelors; they have their own idea of what they want to watch for entertainment. When these guys watch *Bambi* it's not the same *Bambi* you and I knew as kids, if you know what I mean."

"Gotcha. My buddy Mike and I will be over Saturday morning about ten if that's OK with you."

"Perfect. I'll be here all morning doing inventory."

(Next Saturday.)

"OK, Clay. That should do it. We've tested your VCR hookup several times, and it works just fine."

"Andy, I want to thank you and Mike for setting this all up for us. Now my customers can watch their favorite movies right here at the club. I do want you guys to know that beers are on the house any time you drop by. One question, though."

"Shoot."

"What's that other box you added to the setup? I don't remember unpacking it. That's not one of ours, is it?"

"Oh, don't worry about that. It's a little something we added to filter out the line noise. It'll keep the noise from cluttering up your picture."

"Oh, OK, that's great. Thanks."

Once beyond earshot of the club, Mike turned to Andy and asked, "Do you think we should have told him the real purpose of our little box?"

"No, he'll figure it out soon enough."

Four weeks later, a conversation in Kwaj's military headquarters between the island's commanding officer and his immediate subordinate:

"John?"

"Yes, Colonel?"

"Do we have a TV station on this island?"

"No sir. Why do you ask?"

"I'm sure I saw what looked like homemade TV antennas atop several of the trailers. I spotted at least three of these things in the housing area on my way in last week and maybe a dozen more this morning. Could those be some new-fangled stuff the ham operators are experimenting with?"

"No sir. That was my first thought too—then I checked around a bit."

"What did you find out?"

"Well sir. I believe it may have something to do with the bachelors' club and their new VHS tape machine.  You know what type of movies those lonely guys they like to watch."

"Explain."

(He does.)

"Oh."

# 35

# MARSHALLESE NAVIGATION

Our little band of five seafaring adventurers had set off on our chartered Marshallese ketch to visit several of the southernmost Marshall Islands. We were looking forward to being the first tourists to some of these remote areas since my officemate had made a similar trip two years earlier. I hoped to be able to observe firsthand some of the ancient Marshallese navigation methods—methods I had only heard about, methods I was not positive were still in use.

The thin moon was low in the sky and gave off very little light when the captain and owner, Captain Felix DeBrum, perched himself over the bow of his forty-eight foot ketch, the *Louisa*, to ponder the waves.

"Ten degrees to the left!"

The helmsman complied.

"No, no. That's too far!"

The helmsman readjusted the wheel in the opposite direction—about half as far as before.

"OK, a little farther to the right!"

The helmsman then made what he hoped would be the last correction.

"Hold it right there. Whatever the compass reads, keep it that way."

Felix lingered there a little longer studying the wave patterns and the way his boat responded to the larger swells that he could feel but not directly observe.

After ten minutes he was satisfied and issued one last command to the helmsman.

"It's midnight, so I'm going below to get some rest. What's your compass heading?"

"243 degrees."

"Good. Hold that heading for the rest of the night. It will bring us just south of Makin; then after the sun rises, we'll come about and sail north into the lagoon."

Then he popped below for some sleep.

Felix didn't set his course based on his absolute compass reading; although his compass worked, it was constantly out of calibration. In this remote part of the ocean, it was virtually impossible to keep a compass calibrated. It was useful for changing a course a given amount or for holding on course once set, but it could not be relied upon to establish an absolute heading.

Felix had successfully navigated these waters for decades by studying the stars, reading the waves and, when it worked at all, using his compass (sometimes it would stick and be of no help).* He was the only Marshallese captain who had never put his ship on a reef in the last two decades. He was The Man when it came to Marshallese navigation.

Four hours later, just prior to sunrise, Felix sprang from below, raced aft, and grabbed control of the wheel from the helmsman. He gave it a quick spin forcing the ship to turn ninety degrees starboard.

Ten minutes later, the glow in the east from the pending sunrise was enough to outline a long reef to which we were now running parallel. It then became clear to all of us who were sleeping on the deck (too many cockroaches below) that had he delayed his action another fifteen minutes, we would have been firmly ensconced on the reef. His perfect record would have been over.

So where did Felix go wrong? He didn't. The helmsman made the error. Felix, sleeping below, was disturbed by the boat not rocking the way it should. This "wrong motion" made him aware that we were in immediate danger.

While Felix gave his heading direction to the helmsman, the helmsman had been sipping coffee from his mug, which he then set down close to the compass during the final correction. Unbeknownest to everyone at the time, including the helmsman, his mug was metallic with just enough magnetic pull to deflect the compass five to ten degrees. Later, when he moved the cup, the compass changed and the helmsman altered our course accordingly.

## THREE FOR THREE ISN'T BAD (AS TOLD BY PHIL)

I shared the above story with Phil, a friend who one-upped me. He had taken two *Louisa* trips, one to the south islands similar to my own and a second to the northwestern region of the Marshall Islands, including Likiep, Felix's home atoll of sixty-five islands. Phil confirmed Captain Felix DeBrum's navigation skills by relating to me two additional eyewitness accounts—with no compass, only the waves and a few stars.

"My first story is similar to your own," Phil related. "Felix studied the waves in great detail for a good fifteen minutes while straddling the port gunwales. He then instructed his helmsman to set course based on his reading of the wave patterns.

"Next morning when he came on deck, he found that our destination island was nowhere in sight and his helmsman fast asleep. It was totally overcast, so with no compass, the outlook for our little band of adventurers did not look promising.

"Remarkably, Felix did not reprehend the helmsman but positioned himself astride the gunwale of the boat once again. He stared directly down into the water and every few minutes gave the helmsman new course corrections. While my fellow passengers and I exchanged small talk to the effect of, 'Not to worry, he'll figure it out,' our simultaneous nervous glances conveyed, 'WE'RE ALL GOING-TA DIE!!'

"Three hours later with Felix's eyes still fixed straight downward, our destination island came into view straight ahead of us.

"Felix got up, grinned, and disappeared below without a word."

## Wait! There's More! (As told by Phil)

"Three days later we got off to a late start for our next destination and encountered strong headwinds (power was strictly by
diesel). By late afternoon it was clear we would not arrive until well
after dark in the evening with no supporting moon.

"Around ten that night, Felix once again took up his post sitting
on the midship gunwale and stared straight down, commanding
small adjustments to the helmsman every few minutes. We cleared
the pass and reached our mooring by eleven thirty at night. Two
mornings later when we for left home, I noticed that the channel we negotiated two nights earlier was at most twenty feet wider
than our little ship."

After Phil and I compared notes, we decided that Felix was
either an incredibly gifted captain, invoked magic, or was from
another world. In any event, we concluded, three out of three isn't
bad.

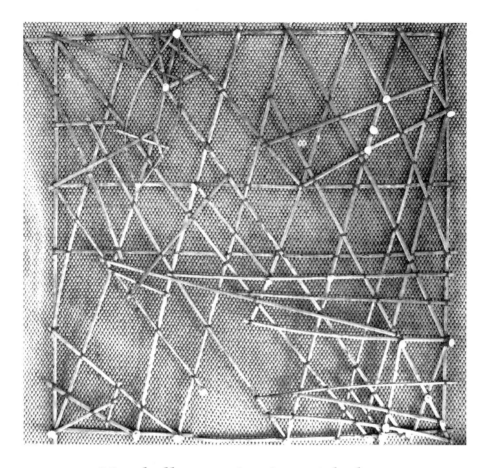

## Marshallese navigation stick chart

*Interference patterns generated by the interaction of the long-wavelength waves (referred to as the swell) as they passed by the various islands were recorded on navigation *stick charts* by the olden Marshallese navigators. These charts, typically two by three feet, were made by tying quarter-inch-wide bamboo slats together to represent the wave patterns. Cowry shells were placed on a chart to represent the various island locations. There are no standard stick charts, as each family of navigators preferred their own interpretation of these patterns. Above is a photo of author's souvenir stick chart.

# 36

# THE GAZILLION-DOLLAR ISLAND

## Antimissile Defense 101

Perhaps referring to Kwajalein as a "gazillion-dollar installation" is an exaggeration but not by much. Every newcomer is struck by the large number of radars, telescopes, scientific cameras, and the large number of half-finished, strange sci-fi looking structures. Nearly all of these sensors are devoted to missile-reentry physics. In the late 1960s, the entire island's population of five thousand, including three thousand bachelors, was there in one capacity or another to support this research. Add in the several hundred Marshallese commuting from Ebeye, off-island logistic support, and the personnel working on the programs Stateside, and we're talking big bucks.

### THE BASICS

The downrange end of the Pacific Missile Test Range was mostly based on Kwajalein Island with some mid-trajectory support from Hawaii. Test missiles were launched from the Vandenberg Air Force Base in California or from submerged submarines into low orbits and would reenter a few miles offshore from Kwajalein in one of several designated splashdown zones. During reentry the whole slew of state-of-the-art radars and optical sensors took measurements on the dummy warhead's reentry characteristics to provide data useful for designing antimissile defense systems.

It's the offense/defense game that the Defense Department (or is it the Offense/Defense Department?) continually played to upgrade their designs each year. It went something like this:

**Offense**: We are firing a missile at you, and you will not be able to defend against us.

**Defense**: Not so. Our radars see your warhead, so we will be able to intercept it before it gets here.

A year later.

**Offense**: Aha! No you won't. We are sending twenty balloons surrounding the warhead that look just like warheads to your radars, so you can't find the actual warhead.

**Defense**: Wrong again. We are now combining the signals from radars employing multiple signal types, enabling us to differentiate between balloons and a warhead.

Next few offense/defense iterations:

**Offense**: Hide warhead inside radar-reflecting clouds of aluminum foil chaff.

**Defense**: Wait until chaff cloud reaches 300,000 feet, where it is flattened by the atmosphere. Shift final detection to just under reentry elevation sans chaff.

**Offense**: Add large number of small decoys that reflect radar signals just like warheads do (same radar cross sections) and pass through the atmosphere in the same manner (same drag coefficient).

**Defense**: No problem, use optics. A heavy warhead glows and emits more light than a decoy.

**Offense**: Design warhead ablative outer surface to quench radiation (reduce glow), denying optical differentiation.

**Defense**: Measure energy (air turbulence) transferred into warhead's wake during deceleration by using advanced signal-processing techniques (Fast Fourier Transforms).

I'm sure another dozen offense/defense iterations have transpired since I left the program forty years ago, particularly as high-powered lasers have evolved.

In summary, Offense is given the task of designing a weapon system that will successfully deliver a warhead to a specific target, and Defense is given the task of designing an antimissile system that prevents Offense from achieving its goal. The test range gives both Offense and Defense a test bed to check out their newest and greatest ideas.

I was working on the Defense side. Our ultimate goal was to collect data that could identify anything heavy: *if it's heavy, it's dangerous.* Sending an accompanying heavy decoy makes no sense. It would be just as easy to replace it with a second warhead. Also, employing a larger rocket to carry a heavy decoy does get expensive.

**Construction of TRADEX on Roi-Namur**

**Roi-Namur TRADEX and optical-sensor plane from Hawaii**

## Launch of intercept missile from Kwajalein

## Horizontal trails: California warhead plus trailing decoys. Vertical trails: Kwaj launched interceptor

# 37

# RESERVED FOR THE COLONEL

When Kwajalein's CO (commanding officer—we referred to him simply as *The Colonel*) left for his yearly leave, the lieutenant colonel, second in command, became acting CO and assumed all of the CO's duties.

A few days after his boss's departure, the acting CO became annoyed that he was unable to find a parking spot close to the entrance of the PX (fondly referred to as Safeway). He decided that such a travesty should not go unaddressed.

He relished his new, albeit temporary, power and exercised it to provide a pleasant surprise for his boss upon his return. To this end, he ordered "Reserved for Colonel" parking spots established in front of all retail outlets and all major facilities.

When The Colonel returned, he publically informed his senior officers that while he appreciated their show of respect, adding CO-reserved parking signs was not really necessary. He wanted to give the island residents the impression that he was more egalitarian than they gave him credit for and spread the word that it was not he who had commandeered these parking spots. Those were his words, but his actions belied them as he left the signs in place. "Oh well, since the signs are already there..."

A particularly sore point with those few residents who had access to shared vehicles was the fact that all of his reserved parking spots were double width, eliminating two of typically six spaces at a clip. A rumor quickly spread that he had requested his subordinate to take this action while he was away so he could appear uninvolved.

The Colonel did have one of the signs removed a few weeks later, about a minute after he heard that there was a popular joke circulating the island to the effect of, "The colonel must really get soused if he needs a double-wide spot in front of the liquor store."

A month later there was a large social function at the Yokwe Yuk Club (club for officers and officer equivalents) hosted by the army for The Colonel's departure as CO of Kwajalein.

The men's room had three urinals, over one of which had been attached a large sign in bright red letters, which read, "Reserved for Colonel." Humor was never lacking on Kwajalein. I was not able to confirm the rumor that this urinal, as one might expect, was a double wide.

**Reserved for the colonel**

# 38

# GETTING AROUND

Even though Kwaj is a small island of nine hundred or so acres (equivalent to only five hundred acres after the 6,700-foot runway, the tarmac, the water catchment basin, the outdoor theater, and the nine-hole golf course are subtracted), the populace of five thousand still had to get around to accommodate their routines. This posed a problem during periods of heavy rain and strong winds or when the unforgiving noon sun made it incredibly unpleasant to be out and about for more than a few minutes.

Various modes of transportation provided to address the residents' needs were as follows.

## CAR

All the cars on the island were white to minimize heat absorption; all were the same make, most likely a result of a low-bidder procurement process and the need to standardize maintenance requirements.

The commonality of the car make/color did pose a problem near the end of a company party late one evening. Joe and his wife, Jean, left the party as it began to wind down, got into what they thought was the car assigned to them for that weekend, and started to drive home. Before Joe and his wife actually reached their house, however, they were pulled over, arrested, and hauled down to security headquarters on suspicion of car theft—a rather rare event on Kwaj. After all, with less than five miles of roads, where would a car thief go? Getting it to Mexico to sell it for spare parts would pose quite a challenge.

"OK sir, can you show me your license?"

"Of course not. Driver's licenses aren't required on Kwajalein."

"Oh. Then, some other form of identification?"

"No. No one carries identification here except for their badge when they go into work. Anyhow, what's the problem? I wasn't speeding."

"I'll ask the questions if you don't mind. What is your name?"

"Joe Thompson."

"Headquarters? Hello, headquarters? This is Sergeant Laner. Come in please. Over."

"This is headquarters. Go ahead, Sergeant. Over."

"We've apprehended the suspect…"

Suspect? Joe thought. What suspect? Did someone get murdered? Who's the suspect?

"He claims his name is Joe Thompson. Could you run a check to see if there is a Joe Thompson living on the island?

"And," Joe couldn't help but interject, "you'd better check on his moll, Jean Thompson, who's sitting next to him holding suspicious leftovers."

The sergeant glared at him.

"Just following procedures, sir. If you will please follow me to security headquarters."

On the way to headquarters, Joe kept thinking to himself,

These guys have watched way too many episodes of *Hawaii Five O*. Oh well, what can you expect on an island where almost nothing happens—has to be the most boring job here, and I finally represent something exciting.

Let me see if I can figure out what they are thinking. Ah, got it. My wife and I snuck onto the island by swimming over from Ebeye so we could steal a rusted-out Ford with a book value less than $1,000, passing up $2,000 stereo sets in about half the houses here.

Vic, Joe's boss (and one of the site managers), left the party less than a minute after Joe's departure and found his car missing. He knew exactly where he had parked and the identity of the contents in the backseat. None of the remaining cars fit these conditions. He immediately contacted security to report his car stolen.

Security was under pressure for flubbing how they had handled a few recent high-profile (albeit minor) events and were anxious to redeem themselves, so they got right on it.

When Vic met Joe at security headquarters, both immediately realized the problem. The source of the problem was too much commonality in the cars—to the point that a few keys actually fit more than one vehicle. Thus when Joe's key started Vic's car, he had no reason to suspect that he was leaving in the wrong car.

Altogether, there were perhaps three dozen cars allocated to various companies besides work vehicles. Each site manager had his own car, while each department head had one he shared with his staff.

The army officers were assigned the most vehicles per capita. None of the personnel from our company begrudged them this extra perk, as they earned less than half our incomes and had to pay income tax to boot. A little increase in prestige helped them bear this benefit disparity.

## Taxi

Take a boxy delivery truck with no side windows, remove the back doors, and line both sides with a wooden plank (no back) and you have a Kwaj taxi. I always thought of these taxis more as paddy wagons than taxis, but they sufficed. Actually, paddy wagons would have been more comfortable. No one could ever accuse the government of wasting money by providing us with overly plush transportation. During the rainy season. the four feet at the rear were unusable, as they were always drenched by water blown in by strong winds, but it was still dryer than walking.

The dispatching of taxis was well coordinated and the response time quite acceptable. I personally avoided them except to attend formal events (walking and arriving soaked would not have been good form). The upside was that no taxi ride was longer than a mile.

## Bus

When it was inconvenient for me to ride a bike, I preferred to take the continuously looping bus rather than call a taxi. The

Marshallese workers were the primary bus riders, but a few of us non-Marshallese utilized them as well. I'm not sure why I preferred the bus to the taxi, but perhaps I felt less dependent on others (the dispatcher).

## BIKE

Bikes were the primary mode of transportation on Kwajalein. With very few exceptions, everyone rode a bike without giving it a second thought. Even during rainy season, the showers were short most of the time and inflicted minimum inconvenience.

To my knowledge, the stories that pregnant women on Kwajalein would ride their bikes to the hospital, have their babies, and then return home with their newborns ensconced comfortably in their basket a few hours later have never been verified—though I wouldn't bet against it.

My personal, liberally rusted, fat-tired bike had an overly wide, metal wire basket attached to the handlebars and two small pegs projecting from the back wheel hubs. My youngest two daughters, Lisa, not quite four, and Mandy, barely two, could just squeeze into this basket if they faced each other and intertwined their legs. My oldest daughter, Julie, six, would then balance on the rear fender with most of her weight supported by the pegs. It was the closest thing to riding in the family car we could come up with.

Fully loaded, we would be off to explore the whole island at will—frequent stops for ice cream seemed to be a mandatory part of this routine. We easily could have blended in with the traffic scene of any major third world city during rush hour.

The girls thought this was normal and I guess, for us, it was.

## FERRY

It was a very serious offense for a Marshallese to miss the day's last ferry to Ebeye. Predictably, a few stragglers would often be seen running at top speed to just make it by "jumping the gap" as the ferry pulled away from the pier.

One day it surfaced how this "making the last ferry" was closely related to another unsolved mystery. A couple of times a month, a bicycle was reported stolen and never recovered. Both Kwajalein and Ebeye were swept periodically for missing bikes, but they simply vanished.

One January, two divers were tasked to inspect the moorings of the small pier located next to the ferry's departure pier.

Coming up from their first dive, they shouted to their boss, "Hey, you gotta see this. There are bikes down here!"

"How many? Two? Three? Four?"

"No. Think 'elephant burial ground' but in this case, I'd call it the 'bike burial ground.' At least forty!"

Mystery solved. Sometimes when a Marshallese raced for the ferry a few minutes too late, he would "borrow" a bike to make up the time. Then he simply pitched it off the smaller pier into about fifteen feet of water and hopped onto the ferry.

## LEGS

Eventually most residents adopted *zories* (the Japanese name for slippers), referred to locally as go-aheads or flip-flops for the characteristic sounds they made as one walked down the hall. While not exactly fashionable, they were convenient and at $1.29, incredibly cheap. Two downsides were that they would be pulled off by suction from the water when wading, and it took a minimum of two weeks to build up the calluses needed between the big and second toe for comfortable wear.

It was quite common for commuters to carry a pair of *zories* in their briefcases to protect their street shoes should they get caught in a sudden torrential downpour while walking toward the air terminal (I know I did).

The next most common Kwajalein footwear was running shoes purchased in great quantity via mail order.

Sidebar—a couple years after leaving Kwajalein, my third daughter was tested to see if she qualified for early enrollment into kindergarten.

Examiner: What is this a picture of?

Daughter: Flip-flops.

Examiner: Do they have another name?

Daughter: Yes, *zories*.

Examiner: "Are you sure they don't have another name?

Daughter: Go-aheads?

(Examiner marked down "Child does not recognize shower slippers.")

Examiner: Can you name more than one type of bear?

Daughter: Polar bear.

Examiner: Any more?

Daughter: No.

(Examiner marked down, "Child has limited knowledge of wild animals.")

Examiner didn't ask about sharks. My daughter could identify five different types of sharks, and I'm certain none of the other kids in her school could. She was rejected.

# 39

# Hobbies, Recreation, and Activities

When it came to hobbies and recreation, Kwajalein was far from normal. The procedure and organization rules that had developed through the years for military installations were distorted by the uniqueness of Kwajalein. Financial resources allocated to support recreation programs derived from a percentage of the receipts from the dry goods outlet—Macy's—the liquor store, and the food outlet—Safeway. These were several times larger than average due to the enormous incomes of the workers and the limited options as to where they could spend their money. With no competition, everything was snatched up quickly—price was virtually irrelevant.

If any resident wished to start a club or hobby, he only had to get the word out and it was done. Think of it as a telepathic Craigslist. I joined a few of these clubs and avoided others because of my competing time commitments.

## Scuba Diving

It cost more for one hour of diving Stateside than it did for a year of diving on Kwajalein, assuming you had your own equipment. Dues for the diving club were $2.90 a month, which included free air, two days diving off a dive boat every weekend, and even free box lunches.

It was necessary for all scuba divers to earn their certification, but since courses were offered every few months, this posed no difficulty.

Nearly all the diving trips used military Landing Craft Utilities (LCUs) as dive boats (provided by the recreation department) to reach their destination for the day's diving. A typical trip would involve twenty to thirty participants, with scuba divers outnumbering snorkelers two to one. Most dives were restricted to coral heads, reefs, or sunken ships/planes within the lagoon. Oceanside and night dives had to be arranged separately by the participants.

Ocean diving was seldom pursued due to the extra time it took to reach a navigable channel with ocean access and the rougher water encountered outside the lagoon during most of the year. A few of the more adventuresome divers tried walk-in night diving toward the end of my last tour. I declined to join them.

My favorite diving experiences were lunchtime trips off Roi-Namur using a small boat supplied by the recreation department that accommodated up to four divers.

Hunting shells, taking photos, being awed, and just having fun were the mainstays of most divers, with sunken ship diving following closely behind.

## GOLF/BOWLING

As excess recreation funds accrued each year, it was possible to expand the recreational facilities to accommodate a wider range of interests. First the navy and then the army had the strongest influence in deciding which activity would be added next.

The year a new CO arrived who loved bowling, a bowling alley was added; same thing with the nine-hole golf course a few years later.

The flying club had financial support from the recreation budget, but each member paid his own additional per-hour flying expenses.

Duplicate bridge, ham radio, Marshallese Study Group, University of Hawaii night school, kids' swim team (I was the coach), running (when not diving I ran at lunch), fishing trips, sailing, and volunteering at the handicraft store (which provided scholarships for Marshallese high school graduates) were just a few of the activities available to keep the Kwaj-ites occupied.

# 40

# THE RUSSIANS ARE COMING, SORTA

In the same manner that missile offense, defense, offense, defense goes on forever, so do intelligence, counterintelligence, counter-counterintelligence, counter-counter-counterintelligence iterate ad infinitum.

One of our government intelligence agencies requested that my company decipher a top-secret signal they had intercepted via spy satellite but were unable to decipher themselves, even after three months of concerted effort.

After two days of examination, Reg, our best code analyzer, had an epiphany.

"Hey, wait a minute. This looks more like one of *our* satellite transmissions than one generated by a Russian spy satellite, albeit a bit convoluted."

Reg checked with Tom, his contact at the government agency. "No way, Reg. I can assure you the data I sent you were definitely from a direct Russian satellite intercept. No doubt about it. Keep checking and let me know what you discover. So far, no one else in the agency nor any of our consultants has been able to crack this thing."

A day later.

"OK, Tom, I've finished my analysis. Do you want the good news or the bad news?"

"In one day? Yeah, of course. But forget the good news, bad news bit. Just tell me what you got."

"Fine, Tom. Here's what happened. On January 14th at 21:15 Zulu time (international time), the Russians apparently performed some sort of test. They transmitted their results via microwave links back to Moscow. One of our spy satellites intercepted and recorded the poke-through of this signal. [Note—a signal transmitted parallel to the ground from microwave tower to microwave tower eventually "pokes" though the atmosphere heading toward outer space 90 degrees around the earth from its transmission location where a spy satellite can pick it up.] Then, a few seconds later, this signal was relayed to one of our other satellites and further relayed to you guys in Washington. However, the Russians intercepted this relayed signal and forwarded it for relay to *their* research facilities. Then we intercepted that same signal once again from the Russians and sent it to you guys.

"As far as I can tell, the data you sent me comes from the same signal you originally received but took a few extra round trips between our two spy satellite networks. Each time the satellites thought they were intercepting a new signal. It could have kept ping-ponging like that forever if the satellites didn't finally move out of position."

Whenever we ran a missile-reentry test on Kwajalein, the Russians would not be far away with their "fishing trawlers"— trawlers with half a dozen radars and radio antennae and fishing nets that never seemed to go into the water. Their presence was noted, but as they were in international waters, they were largely ignored.

For one test, however, we were planning to use a new target area twenty miles to the west of our usual splashdown area, which at that time was inconveniently occupied by a Russian "fishing trawler."

Rather than scrub the test or move the target impact location, it seemed more prudent to ask the Russians to kindly move a few miles to the west from splash point for their own safety. A non-threatening tugboat was dispatched in an attempt to convey this request.

They were apparently successful, as the trawler eventually complied—but not without an unintentional incident.

The encounter took place during a time when all beer on Kwajalein sported the new pull-tab cans, an innovation not yet known in the Soviet Union. Just as the tug was about to disengage, one of the tug's crew, to show there were no hard feelings, threw a can of beer onto the Russian trawler's deck.

The Russians all hit the deck, convinced they had been attacked with a hand grenade. The crew member responsible for almost starting World War III, through highly animated hand gestures, demonstrated how to open and drink the beer. He finally won over the startled and suspicious Russians but not before they demanded that the crewmember prove his good intentions by delivering several more hand-grenade look-alikes so they could practice.

# 41

# IT'S AGAINST THE RULES

John had been on Roi too long without a break. He was preparing to head home on leave when he received *the letter* from his wife with most unwelcome news—the final demise of their relationship. Its exact contents were not important. What was important was it was bad, really bad. John was an alcoholic who had been sober for over a year before signing up for his tour on Roi. That night John fell off the wagon and returned to his friend, the bottle, for solace.

John's behavior got out of hand and escalated to where he set fire to his room in the BQ (bachelors' quarters), forgetting, as drunks are apt to do, that, once started, fires have no motivation to confine themselves to their intended target. Fortunately the quarters were constructed out of cinder blocks, and the fire was quickly extinguished by several of the other residents.

John's thinking was fuzzy, and he couldn't figure out what to do next—he panicked. He stole a motorbike conveniently accessible just outside his BQ entrance and took off—escaping immediate confrontation. "Long-term planning" for John at that moment was about thirty seconds.

Residents of the BQ notified security, who responded immediately. Actually, it was a good opportunity for them, as virtually nothing had happened on the island requiring their attention for the last several months.

"OK, thanks for the call. We're on it. You say John took off on a motor scooter. What direction was he heading? One more thing, could I have your name again please? OK, thanks."

"Mike, think we should call the captain [nonmilitary head of security on Kwaj] and let him know what's going on?"

"Naw, not yet. It's late and we should be able to handle this ourselves. It'll look better if we call him in the morning after we've taken care of it. 'Show initiative,' he always says."

"Hey, you're right. We may even get a letter of commendation. Let's go for it!"

"Look! There he is. Turning down the road over there behind those palm trees—next to the runway."

"Sure is. Quick! After him!"

"OK. I'll pull alongside. You order him to stop. Looks like this is an easy wrap up."

"Hey you! John! Pull over! Oops. Quick, he's getting away! Go after him. Damn! He's crossing the runway. Follow him!"

"Can't. We're not allowed to cross the runway even when pursuing a suspect. It's in the handbook."

"It is?"

"Yep. Read it last week studying for the promotion exam."

"But there aren't any planes this late. Not 'til tomorrow. Shouldn't be a problem."

"Doesn't matter. Those are the rules."

"OK then, go around. We'll catch him on the other side. That motorbike isn't very fast—should be a piece of cake."

"Will do."

"Ah. There he is again. Get him!"

"John! John! Pull ov—damn, he crossed the runway again. That's not fair. Quick, go around again."

Radio comes on. "Nile, Mike, do you read me? This is the captain calling. Over."

"Yes, Captain. We're here. We're pursuing a suspect. Over."

"I just got off the horn with Frank [the Roi-Namur island manager]. He filled me in on the arson details and told me that the suspect, John I think he called him, took off on a stolen motorbike. Is this true? Over."

"Yes, Captain. We've just about got 'im. Over."

"Is he still on the motorbike or is he on foot now? Over."

"No, sir. He's still on the motorbike. But every time we almost have him, he cuts across the runway and—according to the handbook, we're not allowed to cross the runway, so we go around and—"

"Why are you chasing him?"

"To apprehend him, sir, and make an arrest and—"

"Nile, Mike, listen to me. Roi is a four-hundred-acre island with less than three miles of road. There is no place for this guy to go. Just sit tight until he runs out of gas. Is that clear? Over."

"Ah, yes, Captain. We just thought—"

"I know you're trying to do your best, but just relax and sit tight. Those motorbikes only carry enough gas for an hour and a half. Park close to the runway, have some coffee, keep track of him, and wait. Over."

"Yes sir. Wait. We will do that, sir. Over and out."

"That's nine."

"Nine what?"

"That's the ninth time he's ridden by."

"You're counting?"

"Sure. Need it for the report, and besides, what else we gotta do? The Kwaj radio station went off air half an hour ago, so there's nothing to listen to."

"Are we going to get overtime for this?"

"I hope so. I'm heading home on vacation in a couple of weeks and sure could use the extra money."

John, looking very tired and sullen, accompanied by a security guard, was escorted onto a flight to Hawaii two days later—leaving behind one more "It could only happen on Kwaj" story.

# 42

# KWAJ BIRTH ANNOUNCEMENT

D1 and D3 (daughters one and three) were born in the Boston Lying-In Hospital four years and fifty feet apart. D2, just to be different, made her entry into this world seven thousand miles west on Kwajalein Island. (I never checked to see if this made her eligible to become president of the Republic of the Marshall Islands.)

As mentioned earlier, the primary goal of the work on Kwajalein was to gather data in support of the government's program to evaluate our country's antiballistic missile-defense systems. The program employed state-of-the-art radars, a 48-inch fast-slewing Cassegrain telescope, large-aperture position-tracking still cameras, etc.

A "Quick-Look PRESS Test" report was issued immediately following each reentry missile test (six to ten times a month) describing the status of the numerous radar/optical sensors and probable success of pertinent reentry data collection. Before heading home for the night, my last mission responsibility was to issue these reports (sometimes as late as four o'clock in the morning).

D2's birth announcement was distributed May 25, 1964, to our friends on Kwajalein. In light of our rather unique living/working environment, D2's birth announcement was printed in a format that mimicked a missile-reentry test quick-look report.

# PRESS TEST J-002

(Jacobson daughter #002)

PRESS Test Date:25 May, 1964

PRESS Personnel:

| | |
|---|---|
| System Test Director: | D2's Father Unit |
| System Designer: | D2's Mother Unit |
| Operations Director: | Dr. C. Cunnington |
| Payload: | D2 (Lisa Nadine Jacobson) |

This is to announce the successful completion of last night's reentry mission. Quick-look data and the resulting analysis indicate a complete success in the detection and identification of the reentry vehicle type known as the "Secondary Target Observable Radiation Keeper" (STORK).

TRADEX radar acquired target at 500-kft. range at 02:20 hours with the use of the new "WAA" mode. At 02:21 hours, the ballistic parameters and multifrequency cross-section analysis indicated a large, active RV (Reentry Vehicle) with a payload of 6 lbs., 13 oz.

Splash occurred at 02:22 hours at 8° 43.0' N by 167° 44.5' E at an elevation of 25 feet.

Suggestion: It is suggested that in future missions, the TRADEX radar emission power be reduced at 100,000 feet. The stork complained of scorched feathers.

# 43

# A FEW SHORTS

## MASTER KEY

Gary used one of those "push left, up, up, down, right" types of Danish bike locks so he wouldn't have to carry a key that he would probably lose anyway, and also so he wouldn't have to read a normal combination lock in the dark. Unfortunately he did not anticipate that the tropical humidity and salt would wreak havoc with this type of lock, causing his to totally freeze up by the sixth month.

Gary took it to the marina repair shop, as he had been assured by an associate, "They can fix damn near anything."

"My lock froze. Is there anything you can do?"

He was talking to a very imposing six-foot-five Hawaiian three times his bulk.

"Ah, master key. Master key will work."

"No," said Gary. "You don't understand. This kind of lock doesn't use a key."

"Master key very good. Right back. Get master key."

"I tell you that won't work."

The Hawaiian returned with the largest set of bolt cutters Gary had ever seen.

*SNIP.* The lock fell to the ground.

"Master key work every time."

That's when Gary knew he had been had. This Hawaiian was playing him for his own entertainment.

Gary laughed. "My God, you're right. That's a great master key."

The Hawaiian smiled. He appreciated Gary's being a good sport.

Gary thanked him and left.

## *Time* Magazine

I was thinking about the Six Day War that had just ended that very morning, a few hours before our mail arrived. Receiving mail was always a treat as we were so isolated—although typically it took a week to reach us.

I unwrapped my *Time* magazine and scanned the headlines of the lead story:

*Why There Will Not Be*
*War in the Middle East*

"Well," I thought, "Guess I can skip that story."

## To a Hammer, Everything Is a Nail

The marina workers had their own way of doing things, not unlike a lost tribe in "deepest Amazon." Their skill base was heavily influenced by their own "culture" and their circumstances.

"Hey—got a turkey at Safeway. Let's have a luau. Get the spit ready."

"We ain't got no spit," observed the new guy.

"Watch and learn," replied the old timer.

The old timer took a steel rod, put two bends on one end with a welding torch to make a rotating handle, and welded a cross piece about six inches further in to secure that end of the spit. After he ran the rod through the turkey, he welded a second rod at a right angle on the opposite end to keep it from falling off. Meanwhile, the other soon-to-be luau diners built a fire between two vertical spit supports over a cutoff oil barrel.

They put it all together and set the new guy next to the spit adjacent to a case of beer and ordered, "Just keep turning and drinking. Four beers usually does it."

When the bird was done, the welding torch freed it—dinner was ready. Welders don't need other kitchen tools.

# 44

# MOVE OVER INTERNATIONAL DATE LINE

When I first arrived on Kwajalein in 1964, 8:00 a.m. local time was noon the day before in California and 3:00 p.m. the day before on the East Coast. The "day before" part of the time difference was due to Kwajalein's position across the International Date Line from the United States. Thus, during local working hours, Kwajalein personnel could communicate with East Coast counterparts only three hours a day, between 8:00 a.m. and 11:00 a.m., and with their California counterparts only six hours a day, from 8:00 a.m. to 2:00 p.m. As Monday morning on Kwajalein was Sunday afternoon Stateside, this communication was further reduced to four days a week, Tuesday through Friday.

Communication during joint work hours with Lincoln Lab, my company on the East Coast, was thus limited to twelve hours a week, and with California contractors, where most of the launches took place, to twenty-four hours a week.

After dealing with this greatly restricted communication overlap for several years, the powers that be decided they could increase their communication time by 25 percent if they just moved the International Date Line a little less than nine hundred miles to the west, at least for the part of the Kwajalein atoll under their control.

They determined that the date for this change should be set to minimize disruption of operations on Kwajalein and therefore should occur on a weekend, either by repeating a Saturday or a Sunday.

Rumor had it that there was a power struggle between two local groups who had conflicting vested interests in the outcome and who lobbied hard behind the scenes to influence the final decision in their favor.

The churches thought, "How wonderful to have two Sundays in a row to give our parishioners an extra day to reflect and to observe their faith—perhaps they could work on special charity projects." As strong as this lobby was, they were no real match for the local bar lobby that thought, "Ah, an extra Saturday would let the bachelors unwind an extra day—good for business." Final decision—an extra Saturday was added to the local July calendar. Thus on Kwajalein, July 1966 went down in history as a thirty-two-day month that included six Saturdays, much to the joy of the local bachelors frequenting the bachelors' clubs.

## POSTMARK

With an extra day in July, letters mailed the second-to-last day in July that year would be postmarked July 31, 1966, raising an interesting issue: what postmark would be impressed on mail the following day? A few stamp collectors (including me) reasoned that the post office could not legally use the same postal date for two consecutive days, as such dates were legally binding proof of date of posting. We saw an opportunity to obtain a very rare postmark that might eventually have considerable value.

In an attempt to tap into this oddity, I mailed myself twenty sealed letters at the Kwajalein post office, each containing a typed explanation of the event. A good friend who lived on Roi-Namur did the same at the Roi-Namur post office. Two days later we learned the outcome.

My letters all had July 31, 1966, postmarks—the postmaster had just reused the same date, probably out of laziness. My Roi friend fared far better. The postmaster on Roi had hand carved a July 32 postal cancellation stamp, giving my friend twenty letters with perfect July 32, 1966, postmarks.

So close, but I missed. In retrospect I should have mailed twenty envelopes at both post offices. I never did find out if his letters had any value beyond being interesting conversational pieces.

## Per Diem

The accounting department of my company decided that they were not required to pay per diem for our July 32 day on site.

"We only pay for thirty-one days in July regardless of how you count it."

They lost. They were no match for two hundred highly educated scientists, mathematicians, and engineers, whose arguments were based on per diem for every day they were on site—period. In the past, days lost by crossing the International Date Line in one direction had been regained by passing the International Date Line in the other direction. Once the line was moved, staff would no longer gain a day when they returned, as it had been absorbed as July 32, 1966.

# 45

# GLASS BALLS VS. THE POST OFFICE

"Sorry—we can't accept your package."

"Why not? It's wrapped really well. It'd take a blowtorch to open. Even a semi could drive over it without so much as making a dent."

"Post office rules. Can't accept a package unless it is secured with string or rope—not tape."

"But this is filament tape. A hundred times stronger than ordinary Scotch tape and at least ten times stronger than string. It's brand new—only been around for a year—super strong."

"Doesn't matter. Those are the rules."

"Makes no sense."

"Doesn't have to. This is the post office. I don't make the rules, I just follow them."

"Let me see if I have this right. As long as my package is secured with a strong string or rope, I can mail it back to the States—otherwise you will not accept it. Is that correct?"

"That's right. Those are the rules. And I have to follow the rules. Same as if this post office branch were Stateside."

"Well thanks for the information, and oh, can I have an address tag?"

"Certainly. Here. And remember, no tape."

"I'll remember."

I went to the table adjacent to the counter, cut open my box, and removed one large glass ball, more formally referred to as a Japanese fishing float. All this time, the postal clerk, with little else to do, was intently pretending not to watch.

I next wrote the address on the tag leaving room for postage, and secured it to the knotted net encompassing the float (the net was tightly woven around the ball with at least 120 protective knots). Then back to the counter.

"How much postage to send this package to Colorado?"

"That's not a package. What is it?"

"A glass ball."

"You can't mail that. It has to be in a box."

"Why not? You didn't mention anything about a box. It's tied very securely with several yards of rope and protected by the 120 or so "glass ball" knots. And I have a tag with the address and room for a stamp attached right here. From what you told me earlier, this arrangement satisfies all postal requirements."

"Why did you take it out of the box?"

"To satisfy the postal rules. Why have a box if this works? The way I look at it, the ball is the box and I'm simply shipping the air inside the 'box.'"

"Hmm. Let me check the rulebook. I'll be right back."

Ten minutes later.

"No rule against it. That's all I care about. That will be $1.85."

"Much better. It would have cost me $2.25 if I'd left it in a box."

Over a period of a year, I collected a hundred plus glass balls through various means: found on the beach (five), found while traveling through the outer islands (twenty-five), and purchased on Kwaj (eighty) at $1.25 each. I was convinced they would appreciate in value over the next decade, as Japanese fishing fleets had converted to Styrofoam about ten years earlier. Forty years later these glass balls retailed for $250 each.

I repeated this procedure each Saturday, mailing two or three glass balls at a time. Then I had an epiphany.

"What's that?"

"My package."

"Looks like three glass balls tied together to me."

"Well it started out that way, but once these three glass balls were tied together, they became one package, which should still satisfy your size and weight limit requirements, right?"

"Let's see. Yup. It weighs less than the maximum and the dimensions are just legal. That will be $5.45." (It was $1.39 per ball or a savings of almost $0.50 each.)

From then on I mailed six to twelve balls each Saturday in "packages" of three.

**Mailing Kwaj air in container,
securely fastened with rope**

Everything was going smoothly until I informed a close friend of my discovery that glass balls could be mailed quite easily if one attached the appropriately stamped tag. On my advice, he mailed one to his mother for her birthday. Two weeks later, he received a letter from her to this effect:

Dear Samuel, I do appreciate your thinking of me on my birthday. My heart always warms whenever you show me such kindness. I must confess however, that I am a bit confused. I showed your present to all my friends and none of them could figure out what the rope you mailed me is for.

A week later the Kwaj post office received a directive from Washington: NO MORE GLASS BALLS. I'd sent over a hundred balls without incident—he sent one and it broke.

## ARLINGTON, MASS.

The postman knocked on the door of a friend's house in Arlington, Massachusetts.

"Here's your damn ball."

"Pardon me?"

"Lady, when we got this thing in the post office, we were convinced it would break if you breathed on it. We had no idea how to handle it. None of us wanted to deliver it. I got the short straw.

"I cradled it very carefully between two soft bags of mail to give it maximum protection and drove ever so carefully. Then, while coming up your steep hill, something shifted, the back door flew open, and that damn ball bounced out onto the middle of the road."

"Oh, my! Did it break?"

"I was sure it would. Broken package means all that reporting and all that paperwork. But there's more.

"I stopped the truck and jumped out just in time to see the ball reach the bottom of the hill—bouncing high and moving really fast. It hit a boulder, bounced over the retaining wall, and disappeared into the deep ravine. When I got to the bottom of the hill, I expected to see a hundred pieces of green glass down below. I climbed down the muddy slope and found the ball in better shape than I was—not a scratch.

"Here, take your damn ball. I hope to never see one again."

"Well thanks, and I really do appreciate your effort. Only…"

"Only what?"

"My friend wrote me that he's going to send a dozen more just like it next week."

"Thanks for telling me—now I know to schedule my vacation for the next two weeks."

## BOULDER, COLORADO

*Ring-ring. Ring-ring.*

"Hello?"

"Is Miss Taylor there please?"

"Speaking."

"Miss Taylor, this is the US Post Office calling. I'm calling about the notices we put in your box concerning some glass balls we tried to deliver to you."

"Oh, yes. Sorry about that. I've been so busy as of late, it just slipped my mind. If I remember right, you delivered several notices for a glass ball. Is that right?"

"Not quite. We gave you one notice for each set of glass balls."

"Oh. How many do you have for me?"

"About forty-five, and frankly they are occupying quite a bit of our real estate. We'd sure appreciate if you could help us out here."

"Oops. Sorry. Tomorrow's my day off. I'll be down 'bout ten."

"Much appreciated."

# 46

# MAIDS

MAIDS

A hundred or so Marshallese domestic maids would catch the Ebeye to Kwaj ferry each weekday morning to work for Kwajalein expats. They typically arrived around eight thirty a.m., after the Kwaj husbands had left for work and the older children had been school-launched, The maids returned home around four in time to attend to their own families' needs. Once communication and trust were established, a housewife would become comfortable enough to have her maid babysit while she ran errands and ful-filled her various social obligations.

The pay was standard (another word for modest), but the work was easy. After all, how long can it take to clean a twelve-by-fifty-foot trailer with built-in furniture? Breakfast and lunch were pro-vided by the employers, and most importantly, all the houses were air-conditioned—a major perk as far as the maids were concerned.

Freshly arrived Kwaj personnel, not in the know, had the im-pression that these maids were lazy, as it was usual for them to take an hour-long nap nearly every afternoon once they had completed their tasks.

Lazy? Not so. I accidently discovered the reason for these naps one evening while having a beer with a power station expert sent over from the states to analyze Ebeye's power requirements for a pending power generator upgrade.

"We always check the power use time profile first as part of our recommendations. In a typical stateside bedroom community, power always peaks between five and eight in the evening with a smaller blip in the morning. The profile is the same in virtually every bedroom community I have ever analyzed in the United States.

"Ebeye has the five to eight evening blip and the morning blip all right, just as I thought it would, but what I didn't anticipate was a large third blip in power usage between 1:30 a.m. and 3:00 a.m. in the early morning, when everyone should be asleep."

"How is that possible? Did you figure out the cause of this extra power usage?"

"Well it really wasn't that hard to figure out. I took an extended afternoon nap one day while staying over on Ebeye and woke around one thirty in the morning. As I couldn't get back to sleep, I wandered around a bit to see if I could discover what was going on."

"And did you?"

"Between 1:30 and 2:00 a.m. I saw lights gradually come on in a few homes. By 2:30, a good third of the homes had lights on, and I began to hear voices and laughter.

"After glancing though the open windows of several houses, it dawned on me. I felt like a peeping power voyeur, tiptoeing around peering through windows—just glad no one caught me! That might not have been easy to explain.

"Anyway, women were getting up to iron when the heat of the day had subsided. The laughter came from the fact that these women loved to trade stories and preferred not to iron alone. It was social hour. 'Of course,' I said to myself. Many cultures in the tropics take siestas during the hottest part of the day and shift their activities to the late evening. Ironing at 2:00 a.m. makes total sense when you think about it—especially with friends."

# 47

# KIDDY CARE

## MAID CARE

Mary had been Barbara's Marshallese maid for over two years and was more a member of the family than a typical maid. She was a great help to Barbara, who had a highly active son in first grade and a daughter, Ann, who was about to turn three and was destined to change the world—all by herself if necessary. "If only she could wait until she was eighteen to make her mark," Barbara often thought. In "tell it like it is" terms, Ann was a handful.

Mary was trustworthy, hard working, seldom late, and honest. Barbara was proud that she had one of the finest maids on Kwaj. The fact that Mary was a grandmother gave Barbara confidence that Mary had insight with little ones. Perhaps Barbara got a little overconfident, however, and forgot that no matter how wonderful Mary was, there still remained a culture gap.

"Mary, I have to run to Safeway to get some more milk. Please watch Ann while I'm gone. I shouldn't be more than a few minutes."

Twenty minutes later Barb returned with her milk. No Ann. No Mary. No sign of anything unusual. They were just gone. She panicked. Not a real panic, as after all, she was living on a small island several hundred yards from both lagoon and ocean, the only two dangers that came to mind. She quickly enlisted her neighbors, and they fanned out in all directions calling to Ann.

Barb found her first. There was little Ann walking down the middle of the busiest street on Kwaj in only her underpants, as happy as could be. There too was Mary, dutifully walking five yards behind her, dutifully *watching* little Ann as she had been instructed.

## Babysitter Care

Staff positions on Kwajalein were predominantly held by young technical types. Engineering, a rapidly evolving profession that demanded one to keep up to date, was tough and whether one liked it or not, tended to consist of younger professionals than those in most fields. As a result, there were far more children under the age of ten living on Kwajalein than there were teenagers—exacerbated by parents' reluctance to uproot teenagers from their high schools. Result—"supply and demand"; Kwajalein had a serious shortage of babysitters.

New families had difficulty gaining access to the available babysitter pool, as their scarcity meant each mother closely guarded her private stash of sitters. Young mothers would peruse lists of pending new arrivals in search of potential new teenage sitters so that they could contact them early—almost at the plane door.

Getting a sitter was further complicated by the fact that everyone tended to need them on the same night—for example, when there was a company social function. One New Year's Eve we had to settle for a ten-year-old sitter, as did a few other parents we knew. This was not as drastic as it seems, for the island was safe and distances short.

Side note—I am forever grateful to one of our Kwaj babysitters who thought we should change D2's middle name from Bridget to Nadine—a good suggestion that we followed in early June, 1964.

## Engineer-Babysitter

During my third Kwajalein tour, my three daughters rejoined their mother in Minnesota, and I took a two-year break from grad school. Since I had some free time, several parents of my favorite swim students approached me to house/kid-sit while they took their vacations. The few women who house-sat/babysat for families on vacation were already booked, and my friends were desperate for a plan B.

I took on the challenge—but not for free. I was aware that people are usually better served if they pay for a service than if they receive it at no cost. I was told later that one of the women who normally did this job was furious at me once she found out I charged thirty-five cents a day as opposed to her fee of $125 per day (over $400 in today's dollars). Perhaps I should have raised my rates to $1.50 a day.

Once the word got out, I was in demand. The parents and I would typically work out the details as follows:

- Preschool children, if they had any, would be farmed out to one of their friends.
- I'd stay in the family's house and supervise children in grades one through six as if they were my own, with the exception that I was more generous when it came to seconds on desserts.
- Children grades seven through twelve in my care would hang out after school at home with their friends during the day, do homework, and help out with their younger siblings. After dinner they would stay overnight at a friend's house.
- I would drop the younger ones off at school on my way to my commuter flight. They would spend their afternoons with friends but returned home in time for dinner (yes, they all lost weight). Perhaps I should have pushed my services as a weight loss program and charged more.

Most of them were on my swim team, so staying fit was never an issue.

Twice I babysat families with only daughters, three in one case and five in another (all named Brown). These multidaughter Brown families provided me with material that would later influence my first book, *Surviving Five Daughters.*

"Sara, are you done yet? You're taking too long!"

"Wait, Becky, you're not next, I am!"

"No you're not, I was next in line."

"But I called it first. I just had to get my clothes out of the dryer."

"So you lost your turn 'cause you weren't here. So there."

"Did not!"

"Did too."

Three girls—one bathroom? Sounded like a typical fight over bathroom use, but it wasn't. All three girls loved to cook—especially pastries. They were fighting over the oven. I gained five pounds during the week their parents were gone.

I noticed that the Brown family with five daughters had seven drinking glasses—each marked with a name of a family member. To cut down on kitchen overhead and logistics, each daughter and parent was responsible for his/her own glass.

Two weeks after the parents returned, they invited me to dinner. I was honored with glass number eight; "Lynn" had been written on it with nail polish. It was so sweet. I had been adopted.

# 48

# BOOM

## OOPS

Phil was not aware of anything out of the ordinary as he boarded his 7:05 a.m. commuter plane from Kwaj to Roi. Even when he reached his office in the TRADEX building (beneath the TRADEX radar where 90 percent of the MIT and RCA staff plied their trades five to six days a week), there were no rumors that anything unusual had occurred during the previous night. Phil had no reason to alter his work schedule when he reached his office.

Around ten o'clock in the morning he conferred with Charlie, his lead technician, about the day's activities.

"Oh, by the way," Charlie volunteered, "did you hear about the explosion last night?"

"No, what explosion?"

"It woke me up—around two. Everyone heard it. At breakfast this morning we all talked about it, but no one knew anything. Couldn't figure it out. Must have been something in the jungle toward the east end. No one ever goes there. Security searched the whole island for some signs of what might have happened but found nothing."

"Tell you what, Charlie. During lunch let's check it out ourselves—might be fun."

An hour later Phil commandeered one of the utility vehicles and headed over to the optics warehouse with Charlie. They needed to pick up some special equipment stored at the optical warehouse to finish setting up an experiment they hoped to run that night.

"Charlie, did I miss a turn?"

Charlie looked up from some optical spec sheets he was studying. "You must've. I don't see the warehouse."

"I'm sure I had a warehouse here somewhere. Look—there's the telescope behind those palms right where it's supposed to be, so this has to be the right place.

"Oops. I've got a bad feeling that that hole in the ground, right over there, is where our warehouse is supposed to be. Charlie, go get Mick [chief of island maintenance] and ask him to take a look. Let's see if he can make any sense of what's going on here."

Later that day the mystery was solved. Roi-Namur had been the scene of intense bombardment to soften up the Japanese resistance prior to the actual invasion in February 1944. It was suspected that a few of the 500-pound bombs dropped during this softening effort had not detonated. Shortly after the war's end, the island had been swept clean of the remaining live bombs and shells and declared secure. However, ordinance sweeping is never perfect, as attested to by the discovery of live bombs in the middle of London up to thirty years after VE Day. In any event, a second sweeping was probably carried out just prior to the island's redesignation as a missile-reentry-measurement support site.

Even after all these precautions, it appeared the optical warehouse had been constructed atop a 500-pound-pound live bomb without detection. Bulldozers and other heavy equipment rolling over the sleeping bomb did not cause it to wake. Like Rip Van Winkle, it did eventually wake but on its own schedule years later and with no provocation. Fortunately it chose a very late hour at night to go off, when no one was in or even near the facilities.

"How on earth," Phil thought, "could a 500-pound bomb detonate itself in the middle of the night within one thousand yards of three hundred island residents and not be located?" Phil further mused, "This island is reputed to have super tight security but misses the explosion of a 500-pound pounder—doesn't give me a warm fuzzy feeling about our security."

## SECOND SWEEP

During Roi's second sweep for undetonated ordinance in preparation for making the island operational, it was discovered that one of the Japanese defense guns had a live round of ammunition breached in its barrel. Since the gun was severely corroded from over fifteen years of saltwater and air, it was decided that the best way of disposing of this hazard was merely to fire the gun in a controlled manner. It was assumed that detonating the stuck shell *in situ* would take care of everything, blowing up the gun and eliminating the hazard.

Wrong.

The round actually exited the barrel and impacted only a hundred feet from the newly constructed BQ. No one hurt, no real damage except, of course, to the disposal team's reputation.

## ARMY ADMONISHMENT

An empty oil drum exploded when a Marshallese welder was trying to salvage a portion of it for use on a home project. Although his injuries were not life threatening, they were sufficiently severe to leave permanent scarring. The army, in their paternal role, decided to publish the story in the form of an admonishment to the welder and as an example to others who failed to follow safety rules.

The article's main theme emphasized that the Marshallese welder did not read the safety directions clearly posted on the wall of the welding facility and implied that he was at fault for not following these safety rules.

The article did not mention the fact that the Marshallese welder could not read, nor did it mention that his actions were within view of his foreman, who was in no manner held responsible for contributing to the accident.

# 49

# CORN? NO WAY

"Is this your garden?"

"Yep. I've been planting papayas and bananas here for nearly two years now. They look like they're ready to take over the world—definitely pushing the definition of prolific. If this keeps up, I'll have to beat them back every morning with a chainsaw."

"They look healthy and fresh."

"Here, try a banana."

"Wow, it's really delicious."

"Take some—in fact here, take a whole bagful. I've got more than I could even give away."

"Thanks, I appreciate your offer. By the way, I'm Phil. I've seen you over in the radar transmitter area. I'm looking for something to do during lunch other than eat, and I love gardening. Mind if I help?"

"Love it. Please be my guest. Didn't think anyone would be interested."

That was the beginning of a long and fruitful, garden-binding friendship. Both engineers, one with RCA and one with MIT Lincoln Lab, commuted weekdays to Roi-Namur from Kwajalein and settled on gardening as their lunchtime activity in lieu of participating in one of the other options—jogging, flying, swimming, volleyball (eventually banned, due to too many injuries), scuba diving, jungle exploration, beach walking, bridge, karate, reading, studying, and serious overeating.

Phil decided that contributing further to the papaya and banana overpopulation made no sense, so he branched out into corn.

All the naysayers and self-appointed experts were quick to point out that, "You can't grow corn in the Marshall Islands." Their long list of obstacles included salty air, bad soil, damaging winds, and besides, if it could be done, someone would already have taken up the challenge.

"It's obvious. If corn could be grown here, the Marshallese would have been doing it for years."

Phil made a mental note not to upset the convictions of these expert advisors and funneled the excess of his bumper crop to those who had a better chance of becoming believers.

This is not to say it was all that easy either—but not because of the obstacles he had envisioned. He imported a rototiller from the mainland and began to farm in earnest. The rototiller performed very well and enabled him to plant nearly one hundred feet a day.

Unfortunately, he forgot to tell the aggressive jungle to stay on its side of his garden boundary line. He would cut back the jungle one day and find it had recaptured a full foot by the next morning.

"Back! Back, I tell you! I hereby claim everything this side of this line."

This problem should have been obvious, as these vines (mostly morning glories) could completely cross a busy road over a three-day weekend. A-foot-a-day encroachment on the garden was modest in comparison. Phil handled this imposition by walking his garden boundary each day and trimming back the unwanted interlopers—but this extra labor did restrict the size of his plantation.

The corn took to the Marshallese environment better than he had expected, and soon he was hauling twenty-five to thirty pounds a day back to Kwajalein to share with his friends.

"My experiences here were quite a testimony to the fecundity of the corn and the fertile Marshall Island environment. I suspect, though, that the dead-fish fertilizer gave my little plot an extra boost."

Phil's circle of friends took a dramatic jump during this productive period. Shortly after Phil left, however, both tiller and garden succumbed to the unrelenting jungle.

"What I can't figure out is why the Marshallese are not encouraged to grow their own fresh vegetables. Every time a gifted Marshallese is sent to the mainland for a college education, he either majors in political science or religion—never agronomy, fisheries, or some other natural resource skill. What a waste."

On further reflection Phil added, "Then again, growing vegetables on these islands should be done with care so as not to compete too aggressively with the indigenous flora, lest the balance in the environment be negatively impacted. It's one thing to grow food for local consumption and a completely different matter to expand the process to an export product. Every time we get too enthusiastic about a change, we tend to screw it up, like importing rabbits to Australia, mongooses to Hawaii, and dandelions for the White House lawn." Phil concluded, "Perhaps the one-man garden approach is best after all."

# 50

# WHO IS THIS GUY?

"I don't know who this Jacobson guy is or even why the Lab insists on sending him here. I didn't ask for him, I don't want him, I don't need him, and I don't want anyone in this section cooperating with him."

I was nearly four months into my second tour before I learned of this little speech that Brad, head of the Optics Section and my not-very-welcoming new boss, had delivered to his rather taken-aback troops the day before my arrival. This warning put everyone in his section on guard with respect to interacting with the new kid. I was only vaguely aware of being shunned, as I had a fairly extensive group of close social contacts left over from my first tour that had ended twenty months earlier. Perhaps in this case, my naiveté and upbeat attitude worked in my favor.

My assigned office was in a remote building that housed the 48-inch slewing-telescope, about six hundred yards from where most of the other sixty plus MIT employees worked.

Brad probably implemented his "out of sight, out of mind" strategy when he exiled me to the boonies. It was easy enough to justify on his part, since a large portion of my duties involved calibrating and maintaining the telescope before each mission. In any event, I didn't really care.

When I applied for a second tour on Kwaj, two months after earning my third degree from MIT, I was told they had no openings in my area of expertise but were about to fill a new staff position in optics.

"Do you have any optics experience?"

"Afraid not. My degrees are in various aspects of electrical engineering."

"Sorry. We'll let you know if anything else comes up."

Next day—"We were about to make an offer to a questionable candidate who has mediocre optics experience, but first we decided to ask around and checked your credentials. We concluded that with your reputation, we'd rather offer you the position. We think you can learn optics a lot faster than our other candidate can learn critical thinking."

So here I was working in the boonies of the boonies of the boonies on Roi. In retrospect, I realized the remoteness and isolation of the Kwaj site played a major role in my supervisor's apprehension and paranoia. MIT Lincoln Laboratory found it necessary to raise the perks substantially to entice employees to sign up for a tour on Kwajalein, which primarily involved mundane tasks such as operations, maintenance, and data collection—far away from the Lab, where the more creative science was being undertaken. Once an employee arrived at the site, he gradually realized that MIT did not guarantee him a position upon his return to the lab or even help him find such a position. A returnee had to do that on his own. Thus each employee had to do well on site if he wanted to secure a future position back home.

Consequently, Brad was more than a little apprehensive about his future prospects and viewed my arrival as a threat—a threat that hinted at someone's dissatisfaction with his performance on site.

Brad had hung his hat on a theory he had recently developed, inspired by a previously unknown nonlinear optical effect he observed while calibrating some unique equipment. He hoped to publish his theory in an optical journal to enhance his reputation and curry favor with the big guys back at the Lab.

To make the best use of this unwanted intruder, he assigned me the task to confirm his results to convince the folks back at the Lab that this new effect he championed was both real and significant.

His theory made no sense to me whatsoever, but I complied. My results were initially the same as his, but I came up with an alternate explanation. A misalignment in the measuring equipment of just a millimeter could account for the observed effect. Brad was not happy with my explanation and wanted to send my first confirmation of his measurements back immediately to earn well deserved kudos. My solution—realign the equipment, rerun the experiment, and see what happened.

I was right. After realignment, the results were linear, which disproved Brad's theory completely. When I presented him with these results, he became angry and blurted out, "Why are you fighting me on this?"

"Fighting you?" I thought. "It's just science. What's to fight about?"

He was obviously distraught as he saw his beloved journal article slip away and was not prepared to surrender all hope just yet.

Two days later I decided enough was enough. I walked into his office, took over the whiteboard, and explained to him why his theory could not possibly be correct, using every big, esoteric scientific term I could think of—I even invented a few extras to boot. He tried to follow my explanation but didn't understand a word. He had to concede that I was correct, or he had to admit that he had no idea what I had just said.

Gradually over the next couple of weeks, most of the other members of our section confided to me, "I was sure you were right, and he was wrong all along." So why had they not come forward before this? They undoubtedly feared reprisal should they butt heads with the boss and, working in such isolation as we did, saw little recourse.

The ultimate irony was that by the end of my tour, Brad still had not published, whereas I had published twice: an article on extending telescope calibration into the ultraviolet range in *Applied Optics* and a technique determining a telescope's seven coordinate optical pointing errors (SCOPE).

I'm sure he never forgave me, for I had demolished his dream of making a big splash in the optics world. In truth, I had saved him the embarrassment of being severely criticized by a much tougher peer group.

# 51

# INTEGRITY VS. JOB SECURITY

## His boss did not actually tell him to fudge the results.

George, in his mid-fifties, had two sons in college and a wife whom he adored but who also liked to spend freely—a trait he didn't strongly object to, as she created a happy and comfortable home. He had signed up to work on Kwajalein, as it offered one of the few opportunities to earn a sufficiently high income to finance this lifestyle.

Unfortunately, all these conditions left him vulnerable to serious financial difficulties should he lose his Kwajalein position at this stage in his life. Popular wisdom tells us that the more we have, the more we are a prisoner of what we have, and on Kwajalein we all had a lot—perhaps too much.

"George [head of radar section], the customer [the army in this case] wants us to verify the calibration of XYZ, and I'm asking you to lead the effort. Shouldn't take more than a few days."

George performed his task and submitted the results to his section head.

"George, your results are quite a bit in variance with what our customer expected. I suggest you run them again."

George reran the calibration—identical results.

"George, I can't send these figures to our customer the way they are. Perhaps you overlooked something. Give it one more try."

George submitted a third set of results.

"Ah, that's much better. These results are well within what we hoped for. You did a fine job."

George became very sullen after that. He just didn't look right and for the next few weeks seemed to abandon his usual cheery disposition.

I vowed I would never be put into a similar situation. This meant I had to gain more control over my destiny by either avoiding the high-risk situations (where all the fun is) or by figuring out how to be financially independent by my mid-forties, the danger years for an engineer. I concluded it was a lose-lose situation to ever sacrifice integrity for job security.

# 52

# GHOST SHIPS

"Mission Control. This is TRADEX. We are requesting a one-hour hold until we resolve a possible security breach in the target zone."

"Mission to TRADEX. Hold granted. Could you please elaborate?"

"TRADEX to Mission Control. Our radar survey of the target area shows it seems to be occupied by either a group of pleasure boats or a small fishing fleet, neither of which seems plausible. We are sending two DC4s to get a visual while we still have light."

"Mission Control to TRADEX. Keep us informed."

Sweeping the target zone with the TRADEX radar just prior to launch was standard protocol. Operations had to ensure that the splashdown area was clear of any vessels for their own safety. During the sweep, the radar elevation look-angle has to be brought down to zero degrees above the horizon to facilitate the scanning of the actual target area.

The TRADEX radar beam is so powerful, however, that when its elevation is set that low, it poses a serious radiation health hazard to anyone within a quarter mile. As a precaution, a safety interlock was designed into the radar, which prevents it from ever looking below four degrees above the horizon when at full power. During missions, including the several-hour countdown calibration period, the interlock is overridden to allow the radar to begin tracking missiles as soon as they break the horizon.

During these times, the immediate proximity within a quarter mile was cleared of personnel, and flashing red lights warned everyone nearby to seek radiation-protected shelter.

The planes sent to search the splash zone found no signs of any vessels whatsoever.

"We can't find the ships anywhere. Are you sure we are in the right area?"

"According to TRADEX you are right on top of them."

"Well the ghost ships are nowhere to be seen. We'll search for another fifteen minutes then head home before it gets too late."

The hold was rescinded and the mission was successful.

The following morning, the antenna experts chided each other for being so dumb. As they explained to the site manager, "Antennae don't have just one lobe (look direction) although the main lobe is the strongest lobe by far. As the angle departs from the main look angle, each side lobe gets weaker and weaker and soon becomes negligible—except..."

"Except what?" inquired the site manager.

"Except the back lobe."

"Still don't understand."

"The ships we thought were twenty miles to the east were actually the islands twenty miles to the west—directly behind us."*

"Why haven't we ever seen them before?"

"Last night was the first time we've ever used that particular target zone. In the past we never had islands directly behind us when scanning under four degrees above the horizon."

I personally liked the ghost-ship interpretation better.

---

*Think of how your eye operates. It is very sensitive in the middle two degrees of your field of view, but its sensitivity falls off rapidly as objects move farther and farther from this center. Now add a small, much-less-sensitive eye in the back of your head and you have an idea of how radars work. It was the effect of the eye in the back of the radar's head that they had overlooked.

# 53

# LOUISA GETTING THERE

## From author's recollections and
## Phil Monson's journals

I couldn't help but blurt out the cliché, "It's so big!"

Gil, a fellow passenger, instantly added, "Understatement!"

When I look at a globe, the Pacific is big. When I fly over it for four thousand miles, it's even bigger. Living on a nine hundred acre island at sea level makes it really, really big. Cruising between atolls at two o'clock in the morning on the lights-out forty-one-foot Marshallese ketch, the *Louisa*, with only the stars providing any light at all, everything expanded to the point where we ran out of superlatives. It's just big. I mean, really, really, really big.

At this point the expression, "Lord, the ocean is so big and my boat so small," really hits home.

Gil and I both discovered we couldn't sleep, so we lounged on the foredeck experiencing/contemplating the moment and trying to understand what we had gotten ourselves into. After months of planning and re-planning, five of us, Bob, Gil of Bell Labs, Chuck and Red of RCA, and I of MIT Lincoln Laboratory had left the comfort and safety of our Kwaj homes and were now twelve hours into the first leg of our ten day, eight-island adventure to the far reaches of the rarely visited southern Marshall Islands. We were accompanied by Jimmy, our interpreter, and Sato Loman, a teacher and assistant minister from Ebeye who acted as our cultural guide. We were fifteen in all, including the captain and his crew of seven.

Our 600 nautical-mile voyage through the Ralik Chain was to take us first to Jabwot, then to Ailinglaplap and Ebon, through Jaluit Atoll to Kili and Toka, then finally to Tamarae and home.

While this trip may not have been as notable as an around-the-world sail by the super adventurous that would warrant a book, for us mortal engineers, it at least deserves a chapter. For one person, anyway, it was to be a memorable foray from life's mostly safe and predictable path. Our trip was not a first, for at least three other Kwaj-ite groups had chartered the *Louisa* during the early 1960s to early 1970s from its Marshallese captain and co-owner Felix DeBrum.

Only one other group, however, like us, had chosen to strike out through the southern portion of Ratak, the Sunset Chain. The other two groups ventured east—in and around Likiep Atoll (home of our captain), mid portion of Ratak, the Sunrise Chain. The northern portion of the Sunset Chain includes Eniwetok and Bikini Atolls, sites of the nuclear testing of the late 1940s and early 1950s, and was still travel restricted at that time.

## Sleeping Arrangements

Our sleeping arrangements could best be described as a minus four star hotel—one four berth after-cabin with thin, woven mats covering wooden planks to be shared by the seven of us, with over-flow taking their chances on deck (no side railing) or in the hold with the crew, cargo, and the ship's machinery. My officemate who had been a passenger on a previous *Louisa* trip two years prior had warned me that the berths were particularly hot and sleeping much too tight for anyone hoping to preserve a concept of private space. Extra motivation to abandon the "bunks" altogether was provided by our first night's discovery that a very large popula-tion of steroid-enhanced cockroaches had already laid claim to the bunk area (minus five-star hotel?).

The clincher was the diesel fumes that accumulated to a particu-larly potent level in the after-cabin. Solution—spend the night atop the after-cabin roof. No fumes and a spectacularly clear night sky.

Unfortunately, the cloudless night I had so enjoyed as I drifted off morphed into a heavy downpour an hour later. I scrambled in total darkness to shift my fold up cot athwart the aft hatch under the tarpaulin spread across the sail boom. The uncooperative wind countered my best efforts to stay dry by funneling buckets of warm rain off the sail straight into my bed. I was drenched and soon very cold (minus six-star hotel?).

Although my resolve to sleep above deck had been shaken by this first night's experience, I gave it another try on the next night. Fortunately my first night was by far the worst I was to experience, so life improved after that.

## LIFE ABOARD SHIP

To preserve scarce deck space, the *benjo* (Japanese word adopted by the Marshallese for head or outhouse) and galley were perched on two separate but matching cantilevered platforms jetting aft over the water. Using the highly leveraged *benjo* while negotiating large fore-aft waves proved to be quite a challenge that I'm sure contributed to several travelers' unanticipated constipation. It isn't easy to take care of business when a large swell puts one into a virtual free fall every twenty seconds. Then too, our consumption of an abundance of local bananas (known for their binding power) several times a day didn't help either.

Our supplies had no preallocated storage, so we mustered as much creativity as we could and distributed them into whatever caches we could find.

Learning from our predecessors' errors, we negotiated with Felix to keep other passengers to an absolute minimum—we had chartered the *Louisa* on an exclusive basis. However, as interisland transportation was at a premium, we relaxed this requirement for two of his relatives who accompanied us only as far as our first destination.

On a previous trip, Felix had also promised no extra passengers, but to the chagrin of the charterers, he made an announcement as they prepared to shove off: he had a crew of thirty-four versus his expected contingency of nine and an unnamed pet who turned out to be a rather large, bad-tempered bull. After a few harsh words, Felix did relent and gave the chartering group a partial refund.

Felix was often able to push the envelope on what he could get away with, as the word was out that he was the only Marshallese captain who had never run his ship aground. If one were going to play tourist in the Marshall Islands, then only the best captain would do, and Felix was without doubt the best.

## SAILING

The twenty-nine atolls in the Marshall Islands are more inhabitant friendly than the six standalone islands (including Kili, one of our destinations), as their lagoons provide protection for fishing and for sheltered moorings. Many of the lagoon access channels, however, have unpredictable tides, winds, and currents and posed major hazards during their negotiation. For this reason, the local Marshallese ships were round bottomed with very shallow drafts and had minimal keels—good for negotiating shallow channels but bad for beating into the wind. Thus, most of their ships were diesel powered and relied on their sails primarily to increase stability by dampening the wave-driven rocking. The sails would only be used for propulsion when the ship's angle was mostly downwind.

When entering each lagoon through a channel or crossing from the channel to a mooring, Felix would station a crew member or two atop the mast to help the helmsman avoid the numerous coral heads that lay in their path. Meanwhile, he himself bounced about the deck giving orders in a characteristically soft Marshallese guttural tone. Yelling was not the Marshallese way.

## LAND HO! (PHIL'S ACCOUNT)

After traveling all night we reached Likiep. Passing through the Ainko Pass into the lagoon would have been a particularly treacherous challenge for any captain except, of course, for a hometown boy, so I did not fret over this transit.

We crossed the lagoon to the main settlement and as there was no pier, anchored about twenty-five yards off the beach. (Little known fact—the highest elevation in the entire Marshall Islands is thirty-three feet, located on Likiep. Average for Kwajalein is a little less than six feet and for the entire nation seven feet—thus their understandable concern about global warming.)

A small crowd greeted us as soon as we anchored; word had gotten out. The Marshallese passengers destined for Likiep disembarked immediately, including Kramer DeBrum (Felix's nephew), who, as their medic, was the closest medical authority within a hundred miles of this region. We, on the other hand, were to be tourists and therefore had to await a formal invitation.

Traveling from one Marshall Island to another is not like traveling from one state to another but more like one kingdom to another. One does not disembark without permission from the headman (I'm not sure if this is a legal or a courtesy issue). So we bided our time until Ace (our appointed leader) and the captain went ashore in a small skiff to seek clearance for our little party to come ashore from the local magistrate, Louis DeBrum, co-owner of the *Louisa* with Felix.

The DeBrum family was descended from Jose DeBrum*, born in Pico Lagos do Meio, Azores. He arrived in the Marshall Islands in 1864 as a whaler, jumped ship, and initially resided on Ebon Atoll. He married Leiroij Likmeto, daughter of the Ratak island chain's *iroijlaplap* (title of a paramount chief in the Marshall Islands. An ordinary chief holds the title of *iroij*). While on Ebon, he began a coconut-oil extracting business. He later moved to Likiep, which was under the control of his wife's father.

Typically when our little band of *Louisa* adventurers sought permission to disembark onto each new island, the conversation would go along these lines:

"We are a small party of travelers from Kwajalein who seek permission to visit your island."

"Are you government representatives?"

"No, just travelers."

"Are you missionaries?"

"No, we are not affiliated with any church."

"You are Peace Corps then?"

"No."

"Perhaps you are lost and need our help?"

"No, nor are we professional traders nor fishermen, but we may wish to buy some of your handicrafts if they are available."

"Welcome to our island then. Forgive all my questions, but you must understand, we very rarely have 'just visitors.'"

The Likiep lagoon is smaller than Kwajalein's, although its land mass is actually larger (four square miles versus two and a half square miles). The population of Likiep was slightly over six hundred in 1961 but had dwindled to about two hundred when we visited in late 1969, most likely due to migration to Ebeye, where there were more opportunities, more jobs, and of course, the attraction of the big city lights. (The 1988 census showed a recovered population of 482.)

During our wait, signals and greetings were passed back and forth between ship and shore (no shouting, for that would be bad manners) as crew unloaded the cargo destined for Likiep.

After food staples and cigarettes, drums of fuel oil for both transportation and local power generation were an obligatory inclusion of any cargo delivery to the outer islands. The more remote an island's location, the more visitors would observe outrigger canoes and the less they would observe skiffs with outboard motors.

Drums of fuel oil were normally cumbersome and difficult to handle—but no problem. The crew merely threw the drums overboard and let the recipients tow them to shore, where they rolled them up onto the beach (the advantage of dealing with cargo that is round and floats).

Once we came ashore, we were on our own, a common experience of all four *Louisa* tourist contingents. Some of us explored the island and beaches, some concentrated on taking photographs, and others just wandered around hoping to gain some perspective on how the Marshallese lived and perhaps find someone with whom they could communicate. Usually communication was in English, but occasionally it was in German or Japanese (Phil spoke German). Magistrates, members of the Peace Corps, teachers, medical personnel, and, if the island was large enough, members of the clergy were all fair game for conversation.

*Source: posting by Eugene Kawakami, great-great-grandson of Jose DeBrum.

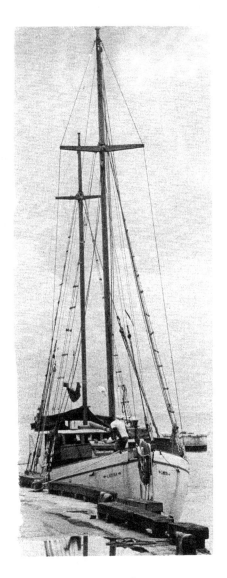

**The Louisa--minus four star cruising**

**Our first island landing**

**Testing the rigging on an outrigger**

**Carving outrigger by hand (Upper)**
**Cooking lesson (Lower)**

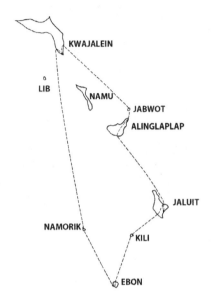

**Our route through the Marshall Islands (Upper)
and Basket weaver (Lower)**

**Young family and World's biggest smile**

**Shy younguns and Proud mother**

# 54

# LOUISA ONCE THERE

## OUTRIGGER

"Tom, what's that?"

"Looks like an outrigger."

"Wow, look at it go."

"Hey, now it's going in the other direction and it didn't even turn around."

"What are those markings on its sail? Some sort of insignia I think—maybe a number? Maybe it's a special identification symbol or name. Can't tell this far away."

As we sailed down the lagoon toward our intended anchorage in the Ailingalaplap lagoon, two hundred miles south of Kwajalein, we could finally make out the markings on the outrigger's sail.

"Those are not special markings on the sail after all. Look, the entire sail is made from old sugar sacks sewn together—and those markings are just the sugar brand name."

I had never seen this type of outrigger before. It was propelled by a triangular sail like most outriggers but had a prow on each end. If the sailor wished to change directions, he neither tacked nor came about. He merely lifted the spar point holding the triangular sail out of its support (a hole in a cross-gunwale piece of wood) on one prow and transferred it to the corresponding support on the opposite prow while heading crosswind. Then, voilà, he was sailing in the opposite direction. It looked more like he was backing up than changing directions.

While on Ailingalaplap, we were fortunate enough to observe one old timer morphing a log into an outrigger. The final product was too small for a sailor to sit in but large enough for him to sit on a cross board while he slipped his legs into the outrigger's hollowed-out hull.

## Sleeping on the Beach in Paradise

Roy announced, "You guys go on back onboard without me. I'm going to sleep on the beach tonight to really immerse myself in the cradle of Mother Nature. It's something I've dreamed about since I was a kid—sleeping on the beach of a tropical isle in paradise—letting the waves sing to you and the moonlight bathe you in her glow."

"OK. We'll see you in the morning. If it turns out as exotic as you claim, we might join you tomorrow night."

Next morning his companions marched up the beach to greet Roy.

"So how was it? Was it as good as you imagined?"

"I don't want to talk about it."

"Come on! Tell us."

"It was awful. Clearly paradise is overrated. First I got rained on, and my poncho didn't offer the protection I thought it would because of the wind. When the wind did die down, the flies showed up for their dinner—so many flies! They were everywhere. In my eyes, up my nose, in my shorts…Then if that wasn't enough, at about three in the morning, the pigs came. No one told me about the pigs! They kept bugging me all night—couldn't shoo them away."

"I'm assuming you will be joining us onboard tonight?"

"Your assumption is correct."

## Houses Made From—

In the late 1960s, there was no consistent housing style throughout the islands as there had been a hundred years earlier. On one of the more remote islands you might find traditional houses made from indigenous materials, whereas islands, which had been exposed to a major Japanese presence would often utilize abandoned Japanese bunkers for shelter. Another form of housing exploited driftwood and wood scavenged from abandoned shipping crates.

Concrete blocks were the building materials of choice on the denser, more heavily populated islands.

## INNOVATION

Among the presents we handed out on Jaluit were a dozen tennis balls. We gifted the balls when we first landed on one end of
this island. By the time we reached the other end of Jaluit an hour
later, we discovered a full-fledged baseball game under way. There
was one of the tennis balls we had bestowed leaving the pitcher's
hand and headed for the strike zone. The determined batter was
using a stick for a makeshift bat. The ball had reached the more
heavily kid-populated end of the island way before we had, and the
kids wasted no time putting it to good use.

My favorite play of the game was that of a five-year-old boy
wearing short pants three sizes too large with no belt. He adroit-
ly swung his "bat" with his right hand, driving the ball far into
the outfield between a couple of palm trees (about a fifty-foot
line drive), while holding his pants up with his left hand. He then
rounded first and made for second as fast as he could (he made it)
without losing control of his other primary objective, keeping his
pants up.

On all the islands that either Phil or I visited, kids played with
whatever was at hand. This seemed quite natural to me as I remembered doing the same in my youth in the early 1940s before
the explosion of adult-designed toys burst upon the scene. In the
center of town on Likiep children would play with hoops (bicycle
rims), which they propelled and guided with a stick held in the
groove of the rim. It was great fun for both the participants and
the visiting observers as they raced and ran complicated obstacle
courses through the breadfruit trees, whose shade offered them
some partial relief from sun.

## FIRST BIRTHDAY

I learned from one of my fellow travelers that we all had been
invited to the schoolteacher's son's first birthday party while visiting Likiep. We were surprised upon reaching the party that nearly

the whole island had turned out for an evening of eating, dancing, singing, and good cheer.

"Wow," I expressed to our Marshallese interpreter, "The father must be very important."

"Yes, but there are many men here who are much more important."

"But the party is so large."

"It's his son's first birthday."

Then it hit me. "First birthday. Of course." Marshallese do not consider a child to be a true member of the community or even of one's family until his or her first birthday—a much more significant day than their actual birth date. With an unfortunate history of high infant mortality in the islands, it is best not to get too emotionally invested in a child until he/she has a reasonable chance of making it through childhood, i.e., until his/her first birthday.

## That Man

"See That Man over there?"

I looked and saw a pleasant-looking man of about thirty squatting at the base of a coconut tree trimming back the encroaching weeds—albeit it seemed to me the weeds were growing faster than he was trimming. There was no one else near him, and he clearly was in no hurry to finish his task. Other than that, I saw no reason why my Jaluit guide should have singled him out.

"He's in jail."

My look of confusion told my guide that he should elaborate.

"He is a murderer."

This was a second unexpected declaration.

"Why is he here?"

"He was tried in Majuro and found guilty of murdering his exgirlfriend's boyfriend. But they don't have a jail, so they decided he should serve his sentence on Jaluit. The government in Majuro pays for his food and other basic living costs, and we put him to work doing useful chores around the island. He lives over there in that deserted Japanese bunker. Most people ignore him as he is considered an outsider, and he keeps to himself."

"Why here?"

"Don't know. It's probably as good an island as any I suppose, and he's out of their hair here. Even though we aren't that far from Majuro (to the northeast), we are still remote enough so there's no place for him to run. It's hard enough for even us to get off island, so he's not going anywhere."

The few times I passed by his work area during my visit, he was always squatting clipping weeds. I couldn't tell if he actually made an impact; it always looked the same to me.

# 55

# Odd Facts

| | |
|---|---|
| Month with highest average high temp | Aug. 87.1°F |
| Month with lowest average high temp | Jan. 85.4°F |
| Difference between average highs | 1.7° |
| Month with highest average low | Apr. 78.1°F |
| Months with lowest average low | Jan., Jun., Jul. 77.7°F |
| Difference between average lows | 0.4° |
| Month with largest temperature range | Aug. 9.3° |
| Month with smallest temperature range | Jan. 7.7° |
| Average yearly rainfall | 99 in. |
| Average Kwajalein Atoll elevation | Less than 6 ft. |
| Average Marshall Island elevation | About 7 ft. |
| Distance to Honolulu (same as to New Zealand) | 2,100 nmi. |
| Distance to equator (same as Southern Philippines) | 500 nmi. |

Bok-ak and Pikaar, isolated from other atolls, have shallow lagoons actually elevated slightly *above* sea level due to their geomorphological configuration. (Wave action adds water faster than it can normally drain.)

# 56

# DON'T MAKE (RADIO) WAVES

## BASED ON GLEN'S STORY, 1963

"Glen, are you up for a couple of cold ones at Crossroads before we hit the mess? Tom won the football pool yesterday so he's springing to buy us all a round."

"One round?"

"Maybe if we flatter him enough, we can squeeze a second round out of him. You tell him how smart he is and I'll threaten to break his arm. A one, two—black hat, white hat combination should do the trick."

"Mike, are you sure you heard right? We've worked together for over a year, and he's never once paid for anything."

"Yeah. That's why we gotta hit while the iron's hot—before he realizes he's invested at least $2,000 to finally win 1,000. Once he figures out he's actually behind, the generosity window will slam shut."

"OK then, I'm in. But first I gotta finish recalibrating these last couple of meters—and I promised Jim I'd take a look at this broken signal generator before I call it a day. He promised somebody he could get it fixed by morning."

"Are you trying to suck up to our big kahuna or somethin'?"

"You know me better than that."

"Looks boring to me."

"It is, but it needs doin' and I happen to be very good at it—or at least I have Jim convinced I'm good at it—that's all that matters."

"That doesn't look like a signal generator to me."

"Actually, it's a miniature transmitter—probably just a blown fuse. I'll get to it next."

"How are you going to test it—you don't have a power amp to transmit any power."

"Somethin'll come to me."

Thirty minutes later.

Ah, done, that should do it. I can't believe this little bugger was so hard to find. They must hide them under the chassis like that for job security. It doesn't even look like a fuse. Oh well. Now, how to test it?

"Mike—got a minute? If you help me test this thing, we can get outta here sooner. I've hooked up the mic to the generator and coupled it to the 110 outlet at the same frequency that your radio's tuned to. That way, I can transmit without a power amp through the power cord and you should be able to pick it up on the radio at your bench. I'm so smart I can't stand it."

"Right. Radio's on."

"OK, now the tough decision. Should I practice my Elvis Presley impersonation? Or just go with 'Testing, one, two, three?'"

"How about something a bit more original? Why don't you show me how you used to run your Link Trainer from your old Air Force days? Weren't you stationed in Georgia?"

"Yeah, fine. But you do like my Elvis impression, don't you?"

"Do you want the truth?"

Click.

"Air Force 123, this is Albany Approach. I understand you are declaring an emergency, is that correct?"

Pause.

"Roger, understand you are declaring an emergency. You are cleared for a straight-in approach on runway two seven, contact Albany GCI on 125.2 at outer marker…"

"Perfect. That came out loud and clear on my little radio here. I assume that means we can head out now? I'll run over and pick up Tom."

"Just give me fifteen minutes to clean up."

Fifteen minutes later, Mike strides into the lab with Tom in tow, but before either could say anything, Jim bursts in and, brushing them aside, queries:

"You guys, did you hear the news?"

"No, what news?"

"There was a strange emergency warning on all the radios over in the US Army's Joint Technical Operations (JTO) building next door! Something about an emergency landing somewhere near Albany. A secretary who heard the broadcast on the local radio alerted her husband in the island's control tower and told him all about it. He's the chief petty officer in charge of the ATC section and he got very worried. He's in contact with the CONUS [Continental United States] people, and they are all trying to figure out what's going on."

"Wow!" Glen coughed. "That's very strange."

"You OK?"

"Yeah. Nothing."

"Have they traced the emergency?" Tom interrupted.

Mark and Glen's eyes met for a brief second and concluded that silence was their best option.

Glen wondered if Jim could read his thoughts about catching the next ferry to the most remote island in the Pacific.

Jim continued, "Glen, do you have any ideas—that sort of thing is up your alley, isn't it?"

"Naw. I just fix the equipment. I don't run it."

"Gosh, I wonder how that radio signal got all the way out here—must be one hell of a skip or more likely, some form of a double skip."

Three days later Jim came in to work with more news.

"Glen, Mike. I just heard they figured it all out. The bright PhD boys back at the Pentagon determined that the signal was some sort of hoax originating in New York, and coincidently a small meteor ionized the upper atmosphere that night somewhere between California and Hawaii. The short burst of ionization gave the New York signal an extra long range skip."

Glen reflected that night while he was getting ready to retire, "I'm so happy these really smart guys at the Pentagon have all the answers. Makes me feel so safe to know they are on our side."

# 57

# MEDICAL ISSUES

Island residents were all aware that the medical facilities on Kwaj were limited. At the same time, they were confident that they were sufficiently equipped to handle 90 percent of the medical issues that arose such as broken bones, heat stroke, allergies, and routine baby deliveries.

One unanticipated difficulty in hiring doctors for the Kwajalein hospital was to ensure that they had experience, or at least some training, in tropical diseases.

## MARY'S EYE

Mary had developed a severe eye irritation. After a couple of weeks, it refused to clear up by itself, so she sought local medical help. It just kept getting worse. After running the standard tests on her severely swollen eye and conferring with his associates, her doctor broke the disquieting news to her that she either had a rapidly growing cancerous tumor or advanced macular nerve degeneration. In either event, the prognosis was that she would probably lose sight in her eye within three months. There was even a 50 percent chance that the other eye could follow suit.

This news was quite a shock for Mary, so a few days later she took a flight to Hawaii with her husband to get a second opinion at the Honolulu Lahey Clinic.

The Lahey eye doctors immediately identified to her great relief that her problem was an uncommon but not particularly rare fungus that primarily affected the eyes of people residing in the tropics. It was treated with eye drops and completely cleared up within a month of her return to the island.

Mary was quite unhappy with the Kwaj hospital—particularly their lack of knowledge of tropical diseases common to that part of the world. Her letter of complaint went unacknowledged.

## HEAD NURSE, OVERQUALIFIED

In the late 1960s, most dependents on Kwajalein would have been identified as stay-at-home wives—mostly because there were very few jobs available to them, not because they had a disinclination to work. Most wives had at least a bachelor's degree and had held down professional jobs prior to coming to Kwaj. The exceptions were secretarial work, retail jobs, a few programming jobs, and nurse practitioners.

Karen, an RN with a master's degree, was the most qualified nurse on the island and as such, was promoted to the hospital's head nurse within a few months of her arrival.

Karen understood that the hospital served primarily as a front-line medical facility, but nonetheless she was unhappy with the way management ran it. She took it upon herself to make a list of the inadequacies she believed should be addressed, nearly all of which required very little financial outlay. She was wrong in thinking the administrator would welcome her analysis. After her second attempt to raise these issues with management failed, she petitioned the commanding officer to intervene. Again she was ignored. A second letter to the commanding officer a month later caused him to summon the head of the hospital into his office.

"Gary, this is the second letter I've received from this woman about how the hospital is not being run properly."

"Yes sir, she's a real troublemaker."

"I can't tell you how bad this can make us look. See to it this doesn't happen again."

The next day Karen received a one-day termination notice with a strong implication that she was no longer welcome on the island. This urging proved to be an empty threat. Her husband was a brilliant microwave expert and as such, was critical to the success of the island's primary mission. He actually had far more power than the hospital head. His reaction—"It's simple, if she goes, I go." She stayed.

Nonetheless, the complaints ceased once she was no longer working as a nurse. Surprise, surprise, the remaining staff, wishing to keep their positions, kept their mouths shut.

Problem solved.

("Shooting the messenger" works even on a remote island in the middle of the Pacific.)

# 58

# BACK TO YOUR SEATS!

Marie's fall in her trailer resulted in more than just multiple bruises. After checking her over, Lyle concluded that nothing was broken, but she was dizzy and so short of breath he knew it wasn't good. Lyle borrowed the department's car and rushed her the half mile to the Kwaj hospital.

The doctors immediately identified her problem as a collapsed lung, probably brought on by the trauma of her fall. They were able to reinflate it within the hour and suggested she spend the night in the hospital for further observation. The next morning she returned home, only to have her lung collapse a second time later in the day. They readmitted her and reinflated the lung a second time. The doctors were concerned that the odds of keeping the lung inflated were tenuous. Their prognosis was that it would be best to keep her in the hospital until she was strong enough to fly back to Honolulu, where more advanced facilities were available.

Now if that wasn't enough, Lyle managed to break his foot while attempting to kickstart his motor scooter the day after she was readmitted. The break wasn't complicated but did require a cast. Three days later they both boarded the flight to Hickam Air Force Base in Honolulu, where an ambulance would transfer the two of them to the hospital.

The last instructions Lyle received from the doctors before boarding was to keep Marie as comfortable and calm as possible for fear that stress would trigger further complications—even the risk of both lungs collapsing.

The eleven-hour MATS flight went smoothly enough, with several Kwaj friends who happened to be starting their vacation helping out however they could.

The plane landed, taxied to the gate, and killed its engines. Before the gangway was rolled up to the exit door, Lyle with his cast and Marie supported by two friends struggled down the long aisle (they had been placed in the back to be near the restroom) so they could exit to the waiting wheelchair and transfer to the ambulance with minimum delay.

The door opened and a lieutenant immediately blocked this small entourage trying to exit and announced, "Everyone, back to your seats."

"But we have to get off! They're waiting for us," protested Lyle. "There's an ambul—"

"Sorry," the lieutenant interrupted abruptly. "No exceptions. I have my orders. Now, everyone! Back, back to your seats. No one gets off until you all sit down."

The officious lieutenant kept repeating, "Back! Back! Everyone back to your seats," as he impatiently watched the little group inch their way back to their rear seats.

Lyle unhappily complied assuming there was some type of emergency dictating the lieutenant's actions. He was particularly concerned as Marie's breathing had become more labored and her face started to flush.

Once seated, he became astonished and had to suppress his rage for Marie's sake when he heard the lieutenant's proclamation, "All right, that's better. Now, officers off first."

Postscript—Marie made a full recovery in Honolulu and Lyle's foot healed enough to permit the couple to return to Kwaj a few weeks later to complete their eighteen-month tour. Lyle wrote a strongly worded letter to the site managers, Kwajalein's army commanding officer, and the commanding officer's superiors to formally protest the enforced protocol procedures that had endangered his wife's life.

He further pointed out that this incident seriously damaged the army's campaign to improve its relationship with the Kwajalein nonmilitary contingency. He also noted that due to his equivalent GS rating, he actually outranked all but a handful of the Kwajalein army personnel on that flight. His main issue however, was that the safety of a member of the Kwajalein community was sacrificed for the sake of rank-driven protocol. He strongly urged the army to alter their protocol policy to ensure such incidents not happen in the future.

The army, worried about their reputation, went into full damage control, eliminated their plane disembarking protocol, and wrote a long letter of apology to Lyle and Marie with copies to all the Kwajalein company site managers.

# 59

# ONLY ON KWAJALEIN

## GOOD AS NEW

The Kwajalein housing freshwater distribution pipes were long overdue for inspection, maintenance, and if required, reaming out. Notices were sent out to those residents who would be affected by the little remote robot doing its Roto-Rooter thing. Thus forewarned, the notified residents avoided drawing water during the inspection and flushing process to escape any negative consequences that might occur. Sounded good.

Unfortunately something went awry. The little marvel somehow missed a turn and managed to lodge itself in an unknown portion of the overall pipeline—result: unpleasantly colored water was delivered to homes not on the notification list and a large contingent of homes went completely without water.

Fortunately, a large number of trailers were in the process of being decommissioned and were available for temporary housing until the problem was rectified.

The original drawings of the pipe layout network proved to be inadequate, with some drawings missing altogether. Numerous test digs were needed before the final location of the lost robot was determined.

Meanwhile, several residents not on the notification list had washed their clothes in an extremely inhospitable environment—black became the new white.

"We think the army should pay to replace our damaged clothes."

Response—"You understood that living on Kwajalein involved risks—anything can happen. That's why you get a large bonus and good perks."

"The destruction of our clothes goes way beyond what we were led to believe would be our living conditions."

"We want to help even though we are not obligated to do so. Leave your clothes with us and we will have them cleaned to your satisfaction."

The clothes were returned not in two days but in two weeks. It took numerous washings in industrial-strength cleaning agents to turn black to gray (almost white). Although the items were now officially white, they were less than half their original weight, and describing them as threadbare would be too generous.

## WATER SHARING (PHIL'S STORY)

Seven Kwaj-ites had leased the Marshallese ketch, the *Louisa*, for a private excursion through the outer islands near Likiep. They very carefully calculated how much water they would need for their personal use on the seven-day voyage (plus a two-day reserve). Their figures, however, did not take into account the Marshallese custom to consider all water onboard as a shared resource—a custom that helped them survive long periods of drought. In addition, the *Louisa's* crew provided their own community unwashed dip cup to draw their drink, ignoring the water spigot intended to maintain sanitation and minimize waste. Result—the adventurers had to replenish their drinking water from local island sources by their third day, and by their fifth, a few spent far more than their share of time in the *benjo* (head) when traversing to the next island. Cultural differences can appear unexpectedly.

## JO-JO THE COOK?

"I've been there!"

"You couldn't have been. No one has made the voyage from Kwajalein to the Gilbert Islands for years."

Jo-Jo was adamant that he had taken this trip, even though I could reference James Ullman's book, *Where The Bong Tree Grows*, proving that there was virtually no way of making this 540-mile voyage to the Southeast without chartering a boat to do so.

Postwar, the British controlled the administration of the Gilbert Islands, while the United States controlled the administration of the Marshall Islands as part of their UN Trust Territory mandate. As such, there was no motivation for either the British or the Americans to provide commercial passage between the two atolls.

Jo-Jo, a frequent Marshallese visitor to my neighbor's trailer, had a history of exaggerating and occasionally making things up to promote himself. This time I was sure I had him.

"Look, Jo-Jo, I can prove it. Be right back."

I returned.

"See. Here's the book by the last man to make this voyage—James Ullman."

"That's him!" he said pointing excitedly to James Ullman's picture on the back cover of the book. "That's the man I went with."

"What do you mean?"

"I worked that charter trip for him."

After a few minutes of paging through the book, I read the passenger list for the Kwajalein to Gilbert Islands leg of his voyage. It ended with, "and cook, Jo-Jo."

I conceded that he was right and had him autograph the page.

## Sit-Ins

Several years following my departure, the local Marshallese staged sit-ins on the Kwajalein Island proper. The locals were not actually as upset with the Americans as they were with their own central government in Majuro. Lease payments from the United States for the eleven leased Kwajalein Atoll islands were funneled through the Majuro government officials. The Ebeye locals felt the Majuro officials kept a disproportionately large share of the lease income for themselves and neglected the overstressed infrastructure on Ebeye, where the rental income was generated in the first place.

## Overpaid or Underpaid (Craig from Chapter 30)

"You wanted to see me?"

"Craig, yes. Come in. Sit down."

Craig took the chair directly opposite the Lincoln Lab site manager's desk, fetched a mint from the candy bowl, and settled in.

"I just heard back from the Lab. I know we've been promising you an assistant for your optics reduction effort for over two months now, but they still haven't been able to find anyone qualified. They're still trying, but there's no telling how long it will take."

"Well, why don't you just hire my wife?"

"I don't understand."

"There is too much work for me to do by myself, so while I've been waiting for my assistant, I trained her to help me. She's up and running for what I need and I couldn't have done it without her."

"She's been helping you? For how long?

"A little over six weeks."

"But she doesn't have a secret clearance."

"She's working in the unclassified trailer. Anything that's secret I keep locked in my office safe."

"Sounds like a workable solution. I'll get back to you."

Approval came from the lab, and Craig's wife was officially put on the payroll.

A month later a very unhappy Craig entered the site manager's office.

"There's got to be a mistake here."

"I don't understand. What mistake?"

"Just look at my wife's paycheck!" Craig urged as he slid it across the site manager's desk.

"I don't see anything wrong. Remember it's not for the full month—probably three days short actually."

"Then it's even worse. Look again."

"We're paying her the going rate."

"Can't be."

"I don't think I could have gotten her any more."

"No, that's not the problem. You're paying her too much. My wife's now earning more than I am—that's not right! I have a higher title than she—more education and much more experience, so she can't make more than me!"

"Craig? Just what is your base pay?"

Craig told him.

"What? Can't be. Our pay scale doesn't even go that low. Hang on. I gotta fix this."

The site manager immediately called the lab and discussed the situation with his superiors. Then he called HR and chewed them out for bungling their lowball offer.

"You should have known better. It's just not professional."

Within an hour, Craig had a 25 percent raise.

"I'll try to get you another ten percent at review in four months. I'm so sorry. This should never have happened."

Craig left satisfied, for now he was at least making more than his wife—his assistant.

## OF COURSE IT'S SAFE

Occasionally my schedule would call for me to work a mission at the Kwajalein optical station rather than on Roi-Namur. One particular mission involved the launch of two Sprint intercept missiles from Mt. Olympus (nickname of the artificial sixty-five-foot hill housing two missile silos) located less than three hundred yards from our station.

For safety reasons, we were the only personnel allowed to be within 1,200 yards of these silos.

The loudspeaker inside our station updated us on the status of the incoming missile launched from Vandenberg (California): "Sixty seconds to reentry."

"Let's go outside and watch," my technician suggested.

"Is that safe? Those two Sprint missiles will fire in less than a minute."

"Of course it's safe. I do it all the time. You can get great pictures this way."

So we stepped outside to wait. Forty-five seconds later, there were two loud blasts, very bright lights, and *wooosh*—up they went.

"Look at that! Wow!"

*Snap, snap, snap.* I took photos as fast as I could.

"This is awesome!" I enthused. "You were right. Really worth it."

I spoke too soon. *Boom! Boom!*

"I think we'd better go in," my technician and I blurted out in unison.

We quickly slipped into the optical station and shut the door just in time to hear pieces of former Sprint missiles raining down onto our roof. Fortunately nothing large enough to cause any serious damage hit us.

Two days later, the army requested pictures from anyone who had taken photos of the explosions. It seems their camera, designated to record the launch, had failed. They honored their promise to return the submitted photos but ruled that in all future launches, residents were not allowed to take photos—apparently the images were good enough to compromise security issues involving the Sprint launches.

# 60

# ANDERSON AIRLINES

## "Have a Nice Fright"

Two groups that could have benefitted the most from frequent flyer mileage programs would have been astronauts (given they accumulate fifteen million or so miles a month) and the staff commuting daily between Kwajalein and Roi-Namur (they accumulated five hundred to six hundred flight segments a year during their Kwajalein tours).

On an exchange ratio of twenty-five thousand miles or twenty segments for an economy domestic ticket, astronauts would have accumulated six hundred airline tickets per month, while the Kwaj commuters would have accumulated thirty tickets per year from their segments.

In the beginning (at least in the MIT Lincoln Lab Pacific Re-Entry Signatures Studies missile-defense research program, PRESS), God created the C-47 (civilian designation, DC3) to ferry the staff from the southern tip of the Kwajalein Atoll to its northeastern tip. A few years later, the C-54s (DC4s) were upgraded to improve efficiency and a few years after my third and final tour, they upgraded once again to 707 Turbojets.

It's been said that if you start with only the serial-number plate of a DC3, you can find enough spare parts to put together a complete, airworthy plane. The true die-hard believers are convinced that somewhere in the world of the twenty-third century, a few DC3s will still be plying their trade while the jets of the twenty-first century will be history.

One of the nicknames for our Kwaj air transport was Anderson Airlines, named after a scrawny, extraordinarily focused, not terribly bright but unquestionably dedicated employee. Keeping everything running smoothly was all he thought about day and night. Although he appeared to have no sense of humor and was occasionally spoofed behind his back, he was actually very well liked.

A second common nickname for our little airline was the Leaky-Tiki.

The DC3s were fine once they were airborne but were awkward to enter and deplane, as unlike the DC4s, they were not level when at rest but rather projected upward at about a twenty-degree angle. They had a true military feeling, as passengers sat along both sides facing each other and employed harnesses rather than seat belts. The DC4 upgrades were a great improvement in efficiency (requiring one less plane in our fleet), flight time (five to eight minutes), and certainly in comfort.

## ONE FOR FOUR

I missed the 7:15 a.m. DC3 flight one morning and returned for the 9:15 a.m. flight. There were twenty of us on this flight. After revving each of the two prop engines at the end of the runway (the usual last step on the pilot's pre-takeoff checklist), we began to accelerate down the 6,700-foot runway, only to suddenly brake at the 3,000-foot mark and come to a complete stop with 500 feet of runway to spare.

"Sorry for the unscheduled stop, gentlemen," the pilot informed us, "a critical warning light lit up on our instrument panel just before we reached the point of no return, so I found it prudent to abort just to play it safe. I've radioed the tower and requested they ready a second plane for us. I do apologize for the inconvenience, but it shouldn't set us back by more than about fifteen minutes."

With sixteen passengers aboard the second plane, we again taxied to the end of the runway to pick up where we had left off. The pilot revved the engines once again but instead of accelerating down the runway, announced, "That same pesky warning light has lit up on this plane too. We're returning to give our third plane a try."

The ten passengers now aboard assumed that the third time would be the charm—wrong. It too had to return to the terminal due to a different errant warning light. All was not lost, however, for after a fifteen-minute conference, the mechanics convinced the pilot that the initial problem with the first plane had merely been a loose connection to the warning light itself. Now that it had been corrected, everything was a go.

Even if both engines had failed on this fourth attempt, we most certainly would have become airborne in any event, as all six passengers (and perhaps the copilot too) were involuntarily pulling up on their armrests with sufficient accumulative force to lift us off the ground. A cheer filled the cabin as we lifted off—sort of like "the little plane that could."

It should be noted that concerns about the perceived long-term safety of Anderson Airlines was one reason many staff did not re-up for a second tour.

That was the most unusual and serious flight mishap I had experienced in my entire five years of commuting between islands. I did wonder about the landing skid marks on Roi-Namur's four-thousand-foot runway within two feet of the seawall but never checked it out—best not to know about some things. I was told that a few years after my final tour, one flight didn't stop at the end of the runway but instead came to a stop hanging partially over the seawall—no injuries but lots of shaken nerves (and a few more cancelled second tours).

## Mandatory Mission

Our Roi radars were critical to a mission whose launch schedule was not under our control. All we knew that morning was that we were to support this mission if at all possible.

The local weather was not cooperating—strong forty miles per hour winds. They were aligned with the Kwaj runway but unfortunately at right angles (crosswinds) to the Roi runway. I was aboard the second of the three DC3s all headed for Roi. The first plane aborted its Roi landing attempt just before touchdown, as a last-minute gust made a landing attempt much too dangerous. It climbed back up and circled to get in line for a second try. We were next and were a bit more successful in that we actually made contact with the runway, but then we too were attacked by a strong burst of wind. The pilot full throttled his way down the runway attempting to lift back off but the crosswind raised the tail nearly twenty degrees, robbing the plane of its lift. With five hundred feet of runway left, we gained sufficient speed to force the tail down, enabling the pilot to regain control and get us back into the air.

That was enough. All three pilots agreed that it was much too dangerous to attempt another landing, surrendered to Mother Nature, and returned to the Kwaj airport.

The local site managers, pressured by the importance of the mission, conferred with the powers that be and came up with Plan B. A skeleton core of eighteen staff, the minimum required to carry out the mission, would take the tugboat to Roi. The tug was the only Kwajalein vessel seaworthy enough to navigate the present turbulent waters and strong winds in the lagoon.

Thus the little band of warriors set off on their four-hour voyage.

Three hours later the winds completely calmed, and word was sent out that it was now safe to fly. The very seasick band of green-faced warriors on the tug did not seem overjoyed to find us greeting them with all smiles as they pulled up to the Roi pier.

**Tugboat warriors**

# 61

# LINE UP BY HEIGHT*

"I've been watching you swim. You're good."

"Thanks for the compliment. Just trying to get back into shape."

"You must have competed somewhere. Did you ever teach?"

"I swam a few years in college fifteen years ago, but then my homework load got to be too much. And I was a certified lifeguard and swim instructor for a couple of summers. But that's about it."

"I need someone like you to help me coach my swim team. I have over thirty swimmers depending on me—too many to handle alone. I'll pay you."

"I'm way out of date and have no idea how to coach. Thanks anyway."

"I'll show you what to do. It's easy, and besides, we only swim against each other. Next closest team they could possibly compete against is 2,200 miles from here. I'm sure you'll get the hang of it in a couple of weeks.

"Look, just show up at the dependents' pool at five thirty on Monday. Try it for a few days, and if you don't like it, I'll understand."

"OK, Coach, I'll give it a shot."

"Fine. Monday then."

I was on my third tour and on bachelor status, which gave me a considerable amount of free time, so this offer to help coach looked intriguing. Working with young people would ease missing my own three daughters Stateside. And I was assured that I could take it or leave it, and the coach would show me the ropes.

What could go wrong?

I arrived at five twenty that Monday but was unable to locate the coach amongst the turbulent mass of overenergized chaos. The lifeguard spotted me and shouted above the din, "Are you Lynn Jacobson?"

"Yes. Where is the coach?"

"Oh, he got fired and was sent home on yesterday's flight. Congratulations, you're now the new coach. Good luck."

With this announcement, he strolled off, leaving me to begin an extended *trial by fire* (or water in this case).

In the next 3.6 seconds I was barraged with the following:

"I gotta leave early. Is that OK?"

"I'm cold."

"I have to go to the bathroom."

"Do I have to get my hair wet?"

"My sister told me to tell you she'll be late."

"He pushed me!"

"I have to go to the bathroom."

"Can we get into the water?"

"Do I have to know how to swim to be on the team?"

"I have to go to the bathroom."

"My mother wants to know if I can skip Tuesdays."

"Quick," I thought, "my experience raising three daughters by myself must have taught me something."

Then I yelled out,

"OK, everyone. LINE UP BY HEIGHT"

This was my greatest stroke of genius ever. These kids had never had to respond to this type of challenge before. They jockeyed and conferred with their neighbors as to their relative heights for a good ten minutes until finally they were satisfied that they had achieved some semblance of being "lined up by height."

Those ten minutes gave me a chance to tell all the mothers and one father that the first week was free, their children could come up to five times a week if they wished, and I'd hand out a flyer detailing my billing and schedule on Friday.

Next I faced "my swim team" and gave a little talk, which I made up on the spot, detailing what the swim team was all about and what I hoped we could all accomplish. I tried to give the impression that I was an old pro at coaching a swim team. Fortunately, they were even less experienced than I was.

Then I separated them into four groups for a relay by going down the line touching each swimmer's head and assigning their relay team numbers: one, two, three, four, four, three, two, one, one, two, three…to make the teams as balanced as possible (at least by height).

"OK. All the 'ones' in this line, 'twos' here, 'threes' here, and 'fours' here. Now we're going to do a relay race—"

My two weeks of "getting the hang of it" had shrunk to fifteen minutes.

The "line up by height" declaration became my "call to order" after that for all our practices. We did mostly relays—albeit with several hundred variations.

## FAVORITE RELAY

My favorite relay was the time I declared that all the little kids would be on one relay team while the big kids would be on the other team.

"Not fair! Not Fair! NOT FAIR!" protested the little kids. A revolt was in the making.

"Oh, one more thing I forgot to mention. Each team has to swim with a towel which I am providing."

Revolt morphed into confusion until I presented the little team with a washcloth and the big team with an oversized beach towel.

"Not fair! Not fair! Not fair!" protested the big kids as the little kids only laughed.

No one can appreciate the difficulty of swimming with a wet five-hundred-pound beach towel until they have tried it. It's very difficult.

The little team had a good pool-length lead halfway through the race, but then the big kids figured how to roll up the towel, flatten it, and transport it on their heads. The big team won by two feet.

All agreed, "It was the best race ever."

Besides providing me with additional income, running my little swim team for fifteen months secured me numerous home cooked meals, invitations to twenty or so preteens' birthday parties, and four marriage proposals—all from nine-year-olds.

"Call me in sixteen years when you are twenty-five and we'll get together," I promised.

None of them did—women are so fickle.

---

*Expanded versions of my Kwajalein swim team stories plus other Kwajalein stories involving my three older daughters during my first two tours can be found in *Surviving Five Daughters.*

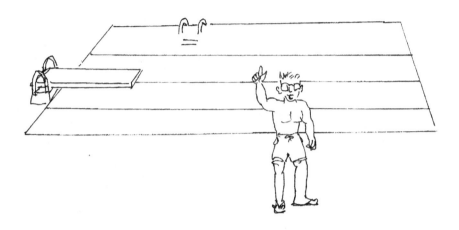

**Lineup by height**

# 62

# IF YOU'RE NOT BUSY

## Last Pixel

"Some of us are having a little beach party Sunday around three fifteen. If you're too not busy, why don't you join us?"

"That sounds like fun. I might drop by."

Around three I decided I was too tired to join and instead lay down for a nap. Besides, I had packing to do, as I was just finishing my third tour and would be leaving the site forever in a few days.

Come three forty-five, I felt rested, changed my mind, and wandered down to the beach to look for what I thought would be a small party of ten to fifteen friends.

Instead I came upon a group of a hundred Kwaj-ites and soon was overrun by a dozen members of my swim team demanding, "Lynn, where have you been? We've been waiting! You're late for your own surprise going away party."

"No one actually invited me—it was only suggested that I show up."

"Well you're here now so do what you do best—lead us in some games."

It was the best going away party I ever had. It kept me smiling all the way on my flight back home.

As Kwajalein shrunk back to one **last pixel**, seemingly the same one I had first spotted when I flew in to begin my third tour eighteen months earlier, my mind flipped from looking back to looking forward. The starting gun had just been fired, marking the beginning of my fourth tour in the States.

# About the Author

With three MIT engineering degrees, Lynn Jacobson joined MIT Lincoln Labs in 1961 as a circuit designer for MIT's solar plasma probe and gamma ray telescope satellite programs. In 1964 he transferred to Kwajalein Island, the remote Pacific downrange terminus for US missile tests, where he lived and worked for a total of five years—an experience like no other.

During his career Jacobson published journal articles in optics, circuit design, and physics; taught several evening college courses; and has been awarded two patents.

The proud father of five daughters, Jacobson lives with his wife in Palo Alto, California. His daughters and wife cajoled him into sharing his many stories collected over the years, which led to his first two books, *Surviving Five Daughters* and *Secrets of a Trophy Husband*, and most recently, *Kwajalein, An Island Like No Other*.